MEN-AT-ARMS SERIES

EDITOR: MARTIN WINDRO

Napoleon's Guard Infantry (1)

Text *by* PHILIP HAYTHORNTHWAITE

Colour plates by BRYAN FOSTEN

OSPREY PUBLISHING LONDON

Published in 1984 by
Osprey Publishing Ltd
Member company of the George Philip Group
12–14 Long Acre, London WC2E 9LP
© Copyright 1984 Osprey Publishing Ltd
Reprinted 1986, 1987, 1988

British Library Cataloguing in Publication Data

Haythornthwaite, Philip J.
    Napoleon's guard infantry.—(Men-at-arms
    series; 153)
    1. France. *Armée*. Garde Imperiale—History
    2. Infantry—Equipment—History
    I. Title   II. Series

    356'.186'0944   UD375.F7

    ISBN 0-85045-534-0

Filmset in Great Britain
Printed in Hong Kong through Bookbuilders Ltd

Editor's Note:
Perfect consistency in the use of italics in this text has
been sacrificed for the sake of clarity. We have generally
adopted Roman type for the titles of units, and reserved
italic for nouns, ranks, and quoted phrases in French.

Infantry of the Guard: History

The concept of the bodyguard is as ancient as the practice of an individual assuming the leadership of a group or tribe. From the Companions of Alexander to the Varangians of Byzantium, bodies of élite warriors, owing personal allegiance to their sovereign and obeying no others, have illuminated or stained the annals of military history with exploits as heroic as the *huscarles* of Byrhtnoth dying behind their shield-wall at Maldon, and as shameful as the Praetorians' betrayal of their trust by auctioning the throne to the highest bidder. Napoleon's Imperial Guards, especially those maintaining the closest contact with the Imperial person, probably represent the last true link in a chain of bodyguards spanning the ages. Though times and weaponry changed, the essence of the bodyguard remained unaltered. The anonymous Imperial Guardsman who remarked, in the most desperate days of the retreat from Moscow, 'We're cooked, but *Vive l'Empéreur!* all the same' was merely echoing, did he but know it, old Byrhtwold at Maldon 821 years earlier: 'Courage shall be firmer, heart all the keener, spirit the greater, as our might grows less . . .'

As noted below, it is impossible to categorise Napoleon's Guard simply into the 'Old Guard', 'Middle' or 'Young Guard'. For the sake of convenience, the present title covers the *Grenadiers* and *Chasseurs à Pied* of the Imperial Guard and their *Vélites*; other corps of Guard infantry, and the Seamen (*Marins*), will appear in the forthcoming companion title, *Napoleon's Guard Infantry (2)*.

*　　*　　*

The Royal Bodyguard of France, dating in direct line to 1261 and indirectly perhaps two centuries earlier, was finally extinguished with the massacre of the Swiss Guard at the Tuileries on 10 August 1792. (The republican 'royal guard', the Garde

Unusual portrait of Joachim Murat in the uniform of a general commanding the Consular Guard—apparently, a mixture of Horse and Foot Grenadier and Staff features. Contemporary engraving after Bonneville.

Constitutionnelle du Roi, of 1,200 infantry and 600 cavalry, existed only from 30 September 1791 to 30 May 1792.) The new republican authorities still required a bodyguard corps, however, and initially

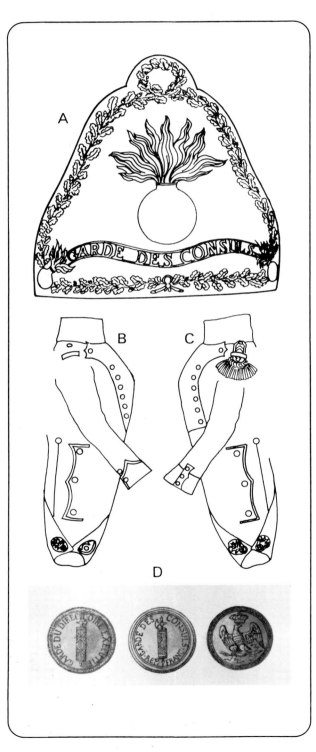

filled the need by using the old Gardes de la Prévôte. This corps of the king's Maison du Roi, dating from 1271, defected at the Revolution and was re-titled the 'Garde de l'Assemblée Nationale'. Described by the incongruous term 'Grenadiers-Gendarmes', this small unit was re-organised again and re-titled: from 1793 the 'Garde de la Convention', it became from the end of October 1795 the 'Garde du Corps législatif'. But the initial intention to form an élite corps of experienced veterans was thwarted by the republican ideals then in vogue, resulting in the degradation of discipline. One officer reported that the Guards 'cannot resist the temptations of a corrupt city like Paris . . . it is impossible to keep them in barracks . . . they abuse and maltreat the citizens . . . some have jobs in Paris and only show up for meals . . .'

On 4 October 1796 a new 'Garde du Directoire' was formed as a personal escort for the Directors, to circumvent the use of the imperfect 'Garde du Corps'. Whereas the latter comprised some 1,200 men, whose *grenadiers* ranked as corporals in the Line, the new Guard of the Directory was small (120 *grenadiers* in two companies, and 120 horse *grenadiers*) but select. These hand-picked men were all literate, at least 5ft 10ins tall, with perfect records, and service in at least two campaigns; they had a 25-piece band furnished by the Conservatoire and led by its first clarinet, Guiardel. From this small beginning was born the Imperial Guard. It is interesting to note that many of its original members, republican government notwithstanding, were ex-members of the Royal army: Adjutant Fuzy, for example, had actually held a commission in the old Gardes Françaises of Louis XVI.

Shortly after the *coup d'état* of 19 Brumaire (10 November 1799), by which the Directory was replaced by the Consulate, making Napoleon

(A) Officer's cap plate of the Grenadiers of the Consular Guard, all gilt—an alternative version to that shown in Plate A. **(B)** and **(C)** are early pattern Consular Guard coats, with the fuller skirts, loosely-fastened turnbacks, and less acutely angled lapels. **(B)** Chasseurs' pattern, with characteristic pointed cuffs and pointed lapel ends—epaulette omitted here to show the permanently attached transverse strap or *bride*. **(C)** Grenadier officers' pattern, with square-cut lapels and cuff flaps, the features which characterised Grenadier coats throughout the period. Both coats are dark blue with white lapels; scarlet turnbacks, lining and pocket piping; scarlet cuffs, with white piping or flap. Turnback badges are orange for rankers, gold for officers, on white patches. **(D)** Buttons—left to right: Garde du Directoire Exécutif; Garde des Consuls; Garde Impériale as introduced October/November 1804, originally in brass but in copper from 1811.

Bonaparte virtual dictator as First Consul, the 'Garde du Directoire' and 'Garde du Corps législatif' were amalgamated into one élite force, the 'Garde des Consuls'. Their original commander, *Général de division* Joachim Murat, issued the following directive which framed the First Consul's intention for his new Guard:

'The First Consul intends that the Guard shall be a model for the army. Admission will be restricted to men who have performed heroic actions, have been wounded, or have otherwise given proof . . . in several campaigns of their bravery, patriotism, discipline and exemplary conduct. They must be not less than 25 years of age, between 1.78 and 1.84 metres in height, of robust constitution and exemplary conduct. They must have participated in three campaigns in the Wars of Liberation, and know how to read and write.'

In effect, Bonaparte was assembling the cream of the army into one corps owing its loyalty to him personally, formed of men who had marched and fought under him throughout the previous several years and with whom his popularity was guaranteed. For the next 15 years the Guard, though greatly enlarged, remained the model for the Empire, with the 'Old Guard', the élite of the élite, providing the final and invincible bulwark: the 'marching rampart', as it was styled by one of its members, Jean-Roche Coignet.

Although it was named the Garde des Consuls from the end of November 1799, the decree specifying its organisation was not issued until 13 Nivôse, Year VIII (3 January 1800). Its establishment was 2,089 men including a staff of 71, a company of light infantry, two battalions of *grenadiers*, a company of *chasseurs à cheval*, two squadrons of *grenadiers à cheval* and a company of light artillery. The two senior regiments of what was to become the Old Guard—the 1st Grenadiers à Pied and 1st Chasseurs à Pied—took 2 December 1799 as the date of their creation, though their antecedents were obviously traceable further back; and it is with these units that the present work is primarily concerned. The Garde des Consuls soon acquired the intended status of an élite, their discipline stricter and their appearance more imposing than that of the Line, and enjoying accordingly higher privileges: better clothing, food, and living conditions, and vastly higher pay—for a

Cymbalist, Grenadiers, full dress c.1801. Crimson turban with white pagri and plume, gold chains and fringe. Blue *surtout* with crimson collar, gold lace and epaulettes. Crimson breeches with gold lace; gold-laced boots. White belt, gilt plate. Print after H. Boisselier, based on Chataignier.

grenadier almost twice that of his Line equivalent—and the superior prestige and status which accompanied it. From the beginning, the Guard enjoyed complete autonomy, finance and supply included, so that it was virtually a self-contained army in itself. In return for such favoured treatment, the Guard gave the First Consul its unswerving and unquestioning loyalty.

Organisation of the Grenadiers was as follows: one *chef de brigade* (Frère), two *chefs de bataillon*, two *capitaines-adjutant-major*, One *quartier-maître-trésorier*, two adjutants, two *porte-drapeaux* (standard bearers), two surgeons, one drum-major, two *caporaux-tambours* (drum-corporals), one *chef de musique*, 48 musicians, 48 officers, 24 drummers and 1,128 *grenadiers* in two battalions of six companies each. In November 1801 the battalions were enlarged to

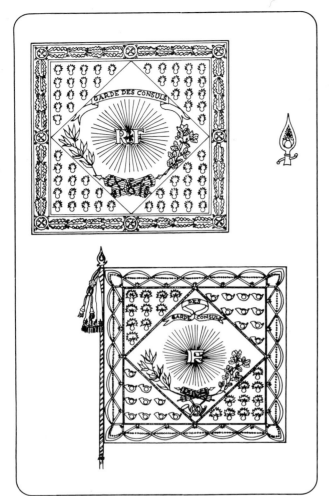

(Top) Colour, Grenadiers à Pied, Consular Guard. White diamond with silver 'RF' on gold sunburst. Brown fasces, silver spearheads, green foliate binding. Green sprays; white scroll, gold edge and lettering. Corner triangles of blue (left) and red (right) with gold grenades. Broad white border edged gold, with gold oakleaves. Dimensions (176cm square) and *cravate* as for Chasseurs à Pied. Blue pole with gold spirals, though Potrelle shows a pole covered with red fabric, with unclear gold decoration perhaps representing a gold fringe along the whole length. Right—gilded pike head with grenade design, also used by Chasseurs.

(Bottom) Colour, Chasseurs à Pied, Consular Guard. Broadly as Grenadiers, except for following: Gold horn below gold fasces, silver spearheads, green binding. Gold-edged corner triangles and central diamond, colours as above. Green border with gold decoration and silver 'pearls'. Green pole with gold spirals. Tricolour *cravate* with gold fringe, embroidery and cords; gilded pike head. A contemporary illustration shows slight variations, including horns with mouths pointing to the right.

marched as if on parade, drums beating, and singing to the accompaniment of Guiardel's band the defiant '*On va leur percer le flanc*' ('We're off to pierce their flank')—music which, as Coignet wrote of Austerlitz, 'was enough to make a paralytic move forward'. Individual heroes were always part of the mystique of the Guard, and this occasion was no exception; *Grenadier* Brabant took over an abandoned 4-pdr cannon and worked it unaided for over half an hour, until his hand was shot off and he collapsed from loss of blood.

The Guard grew ever larger; on 8 September 1800 the total stood at 3,657 men, with the original company of light infantry enlarged first to one, and later (19 November 1801) two battalions of Chasseurs à Pied, organised similarly to the Grenadiers, with the same staff but only 35 musicians. Guarding the First Consul's palace and person tied them more closely to him, and a further mark of favour was the appointment of Davoût and Bessières as commanders of the Guard infantry and cavalry respectively. By 8 March 1802 the total strength had attained 5,376; and this year saw a further modification of title, from Garde des Consuls to Garde Consulaire. Height requirements were now 1.80m for *grenadiers* and 1.70m for *chasseurs*.

In January 1804 Bonaparte created a corps of potential officer-cadets to be attached to the Guard. Gallicising an ancient Roman term into *vélites* to avoid republican objections to the aristocratic word 'cadet'. One battalion of five companies of Vélites of the Guard was attached to each infantry corps by July 1804, styled Vélite-Grenadiers and Vélite-Chasseurs. Officers and NCOs were drawn from the Grenadiers and Chasseurs, and the young recruits received instruction to fit them for holding commissions in due course. Admission was restricted to young men of some education and respectable family, each paying 200 francs for the privilege of enlisting or being conscripted. One of the first *vélites*, Jean-Baptiste Barrès, admitted that though prospects of promotion were 'not especially attractive', it was believed that a commission would result for the most competent. One of the first recruits was Thomas Bugeaud, a young country squire, whose practical military education in the Vélites enabled him to become a Marshal of France and a Duke.

eight companies of 110 men each, giving a total of 1,760 *grenadiers*.

In 1800 the Guard was 'blooded' and laid the foundations of its invincible reputation, when it stood firm amid the wavering French lines at Marengo. A 'fortress of granite', the Guard

On 10 May 1804 the order of the day to the Guard announced the proclamation of Napoleon Bonaparte as Emperor of the French, and the Guard itself took its final title: La Garde Impériale, the title under which it was to rise from a strength of 9,775 men in 1804 to a maximum in 1814 of 102,706, though at the most difficult times these establishments were only theoretical. In January 1814, for example, there were some 17,498 Guardsmen effectively under arms instead of the notional 81,006. This enlargement of the Guard resulted in the existence of three categories of Guardsmen: the veteran 'Old Guard', the 'Middle Guard' and the 'Young Guard'—though terminology was not consistent, and was only established firmly as late as 1812 by the Guard's chief of personnel, Courtois. For the infantry it was as follows, incorporating the many new regiments raised in the post-Austerlitz period:

Old Guard: all officers of Grenadiers, Chasseurs, Fusiliers and Seamen; lieutenant-colonels, majors and captains of Voltigeurs, Tirailleurs, Flanqueurs and National Guards; all rank-and-file of 1st Grenadiers, 1st Chasseurs, Veterans and Seamen; NCOs of 2nd Grenadiers, 2nd Chasseurs and Fusiliers.

Middle Guard: 3rd Grenadiers, including its Amsterdam Veteran Company; corporals and privates of 2nd Grenadiers, 2nd Chasseurs and Fusiliers; Vélites of Florence and Turin.

Young Guard: Voltigeurs, Tirailleurs, Flanqueurs, National Guards and Pupilles.

Units other than the Grenadiers and Chasseurs will be covered in the forthcoming companion title, *Napoleon's Guard Infantry (2)*.

Napoleon's personal supervision of even the most mundane matters—such as the quality of ration bread—served to deepen the reciprocal affection between Emperor and Guard. When the lovesick *Grenadier* Gambin committed suicide, Napoleon personally issued an order to the effect that 'it requires as much real courage to suffer anguish of soul with equanimity as to face the fire from a battery without flinching. Abandoning one's self to grief, killing one's self to get away from it, is like leaving a battlefield before one is vanquished.' This paternal attitude was again evident when, upon inspecting the barracks, Napoleon noticed a 6ft 4in *grenadier* stretched on his bed with his feet hanging over the edge; he ordered new seven-foot beds to be provided immediately, acknowledging that Guardsmen were larger than ordinary soldiers!

The Men

Recruits to the Old Guard were drawn from NCOs and privates of the Line with ten years' service and good conduct records; or from the Guard Fusiliers (formed 1806), the Fusiliers being reinforced by members of the Young Guard. There was a constant process of exchange of men between the Guard regiments, including the reverse process of, for example, commissioning Old Guard NCOs into

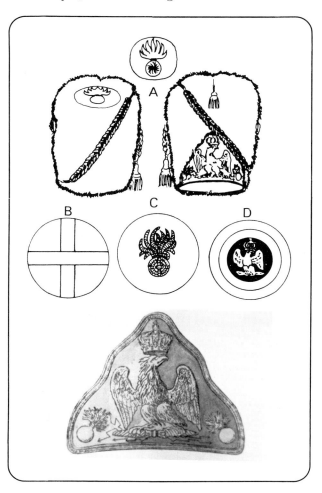

(A) 'Beehive' of the Grenadiers à Pied—the fur cap with the rear patch worn after 1808, and the hemispherical cockade of c.1806/08–1811. (B) Lace cross worn on rear patch until 1808. (C) Officer's version of patch grenade, from 1808, in sequinned gold embroidery on scarlet. (D) Cockade worn after 1806: white outer edge, scarlet inner ring, broad blue centre with orange crowned eagle. (Bottom) Fur cap plate, Grenadiers of the Imperial Guard; originally brass, later copper. Pattern apparently introduced October 1804, though actual adoption may have been delayed.

Officer of the Grenadiers à Pied in full dress, including white gaiters. Note two *raquettes* **on the somewhat exaggerated cap in this print by Pierre Martinet.**

the Young Guard. Recruits of exceptional bravery and distinction, as preferred by the Guard, could occasionally slip through the stringent conditions of entry. Coignet, recommended for the Guard for his exceptional heroism in the 96th Demi-Brigade, was accepted by the Grenadiers despite his lack of height, thanks to the conspiracy of his company captain and Davoût himself (nominal commandant of the Grenadiers; Soult fulfilled the same position for the Chasseurs): Coignet passing his height inspection by padding his shoes with packs of playing-cards! A further concession was to allow him to keep his beard (worn as a *sapeur* in the 96th) for his first month as a *grenadier*. As a joke he—the smallest man in the regiment—was made the 'comrade' of the gigantic *grenadier* who was the

regiment's tallest. So highly was Coignet regarded that he was appointed corporal before he could read and write, strictly against the regulation that literacy was mandatory for promotion; so that while Coignet taught his company their drill, they taught him his letters!

Even in the aftermath of the Russian campaign, recruiting standards were enforced stringently. On 19 March 1813 Napoleon wrote that 'an officer or NCO may not be admitted into the Old Guard until he has served 12 years and fought in several campaigns; a soldier must have served ten years and fought in several campaigns; but eight years' service is sufficient to enter the 2nd Chasseurs and 2nd Grenadiers. If nominations contrary to this rule are made they shall be presented for confirmation to the Emperor before taking effect.' Thus the overall standard of at least the Old Guard was maintained throughout the Empire, despite the decline in calibre of the French army as a whole as successive campaigns took an increasing toll.

Membership of the Guard placed even the ordinary soldier in a privileged position, for not only were pay, rations and conditions infinitely superior to those enjoyed by the Line (and Guardsmen outranked their fellows in Line regiments), but even officers and NCOs addressed the ordinary Guardsman as 'Monsieur'. Privilege was most obvious in the field. The Guard had first claim on equipment and personnel, which could have a disastrous effect upon the remainder of the army: for example, on the retreat from Moscow the Guard arrived at Smolensk first, and appropriated all the supplies in three days of looting which left the rearguard and the mass of fugitives virtually nothing upon which to subsist. The Guard's Colours were kept in Napoleon's suite; and all Line regiments were ordered to halt, form line and present arms when a Guard unit passed. An unlooked-for privilege, however, was for the Guard to be held back from combat as the army's final reserve, much to the annoyance of the Guard itself. As Napoleon remarked at Borodino, when refusing to commit the Guard (which could conceivably have brought about the successful termination of the campaign by the destruction of the Russian army): 'When you are eight hundred leagues from France you do not wreck your last reserve.' Though it was never applied to the Guard infantry, the nickname used by the rest of the army shows a cynical view of the combat record of the *Gendarmerie d'Elite* of the Guard: 'the Immortals'.

Promotion within the Guard was often slow, unless men accepted a transfer to corps of lesser prestige. Gen. Dorsenne, appointed the Grenadiers' commandant in order to hone their discipline and drill to perfection, had an aristocratic background which prompted him to suggest that Guard officers should be restricted to 'sons of good families'. Napoleon disagreed: 'The officers of my Guard had little education, but they fitted into my scheme. They were all old soldiers, sons of labourers and artisans, who depended entirely upon me. Paris society had no hold on them. I had more influence over them, and was surer of them than if they had come from a higher class.' Thus, Col. (later Gen.) Hulin of the Grenadiers, though a veteran of the Royal army, including service in the Swiss Guard, was a genuine stormer of the Bastille and had worked in a laundry. Baron Gros, commandant of the Chasseurs, was qualified by bravery and service rather than fine manners or education. Prone to malapropism and unable to pronounce his own name properly (his dialect version was 'Grosse'), he even bantered with the Emperor. At a review Napoleon teased him by saying, 'Gros, the Grenadiers handle their weapons better than the Chasseurs'; came the reply: 'I'll wager six francs that my Chasseurs perform drill better than your Grenadiers!'

For those officers wishing to remain in the Guard promotion was slower in wartime than in peace, for as Lt. Charles Faré of the 2nd Grenadiers explained, Line officers who had distinguished themselves in action could scarcely be refused admission to the Guard, filling from outside any vacancies which occurred. Faré thought promotion depended upon the favour of one's superiors, leaving him little hope for personal advancement, due to his 'lack of aptitude for intrigue'. It could be slow in the ranks, too, as *Vélite* Barrès discovered; his own promotion was thwarted by the hatred of his sergeant-major, who (not unreasonably) resented Barrès' laughter when the sergeant-major was wounded at Eylau!

Discipline reached perfection under Dorsenne, 'so severe that he made the most unruly soldier tremble', as Coignet wrote. His inspections were so painstaking that four days in the guardroom were awarded to an NCO whose company bread-shelf bore a speck of dust, and Dorsenne even lifted up the men's waistcoats to check that their shirts underneath were clean! Nevertheless, he was the perfect commander, as the worshipping Coignet said: 'He might have been held up as an example for all our generals, both for courage and bearing. A finer-looking soldier was not to be seen on the battlefield. I have seen him one moment covered with dirt by shells, and the next he would be up

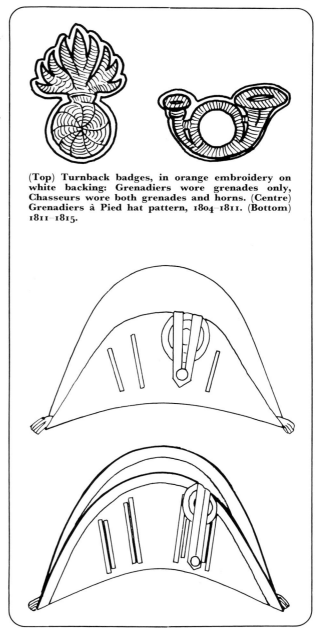

(Top) Turnback badges, in orange embroidery on white backing: Grenadiers wore grenades only, Chasseurs wore both grenades and horns. (Centre) Grenadiers à Pied hat pattern, 1804–1811. (Bottom) 1811–1815.

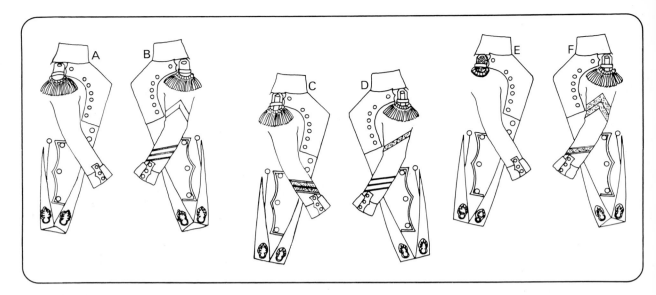

(A) and (B) show Grenadiers à Pied coats of the style used from c.1808, the lapels with a sharper angle than before, and the turnbacks stitched down. (A) Grenadier. Blue; white lapels and cuff flaps; scarlet cuffs, turnbacks, pocket piping, epaulettes. Position of orange-on-white grenade turnback badges seems to have varied, but usually shown very close to bottom edge. (B) Corporal. As above, but two orange rank bars edged scarlet on forearms; orange service chevron on left upper arm.

(C) and (D) show Grenadier coats as worn from c.1810, the turnbacks now extending to the bottom edge of the skirt. (C) Sergeant-major. Epaulettes with gold lace edging on strap, gold crescent, gold *bride* edged scarlet, gold fringe overlaid on scarlet. Gold lace rank bars edged scarlet. (D) *Fourrier.* Sergeant's epaulettes, corporal's rank bars, gold diagonal *fourrier's* bar on upper sleeves.

(E) Officer's coat, rank of *chef de bataillon* or below, after c.1810. Fringeless gold epaulette on right shoulder; coat colouring as for troops, apart from gold turnback badges. (F) Sergeant, c.1808–c.1810. Colouring as above, but scarlet epaulettes with gold lace edging to strap, gold crescent, gold fringe overlaid on scarlet. Gold rank bar edged scarlet; gold service chevrons (15–20 years).

again saying, "It is nothing, Grenadiers, your general is near you."'

With such discipline (the Grenadiers were once paraded up to a five-foot stone wall and, as the order to halt had not been given, they clambered over in ranks: 'It was a sight to see us go over', wrote Coignet) and such commanders, the morale of the Guard never flinched. Always accompanying their Emperor in person, the Old Guard stood out amid the wreck of retreat; Larrey noted that they 'aroused amazement and admiration by their bearing' in the bleakest moments of 1812, 'and they entered Vilna as if on parade'. The morale of the Old Guard was reflected in philosophy like that of Faré after the retreat from Moscow: 'Whatever they say, life is a blessing, and we have learned through resignation and hope, if not how to be happy, at least how to eat horse meat with relish.' The Belgian sergeant Henri Scheltens of the 2nd Grenadiers, after a wretched night in 1813, spent standing-to without food or warmth: 'It was a case of singing, "Oh! what a joy it is to be a soldier" . . . At such a time the soldier no longer has any [worries]; he abnegates life; he couldn't care a b....., as we used to say.' The quartermaster who lost a leg to a cannon ball at Eylau hopped off to hospital using two muskets as crutches, his only comment being that as he owned three pairs of boots, they would now last twice as long as he had expected!

Expansions and Campaigns

In 1804 the organisation of the Grenadiers included a staff of a colonel, a major, three *chefs de bataillon*, three *adjutant-majors* and three assistants (*sous-adjutants*), two *porte-drapeaux*, three medical officers, a drum-major, three *caporaux-tambours*, a *chef de musique* and 46 musicians. The two Grenadier battalions comprised eight companies, each of a captain, a first lieutenant, two second lieutenants, a sergeant-major, four sergeants, a *fourrier* (quarter-master corporal), eight corporals, two *sapeurs* (pioneers), two drummers and 80 *grenadiers*. The attached battalion of Vélite-Grenadiers comprised five companies, each of a captain, a first lieutenant, a second lieutenant, a sergeant-major, four sergeants, a *fourrier*, eight corporals, a drummer and 172 *vélites*. Organisation of the Chasseurs was similar.

The Guard marched with Napoleon in the

Austerlitz campaign, but the infantry was held in reserve; 'it cried with rage', said the despatch. In 1806 each Line battalion was ordered to supply a recruit to the Guard: under 35 years of age, 5ft 10ins for a *grenadier* and 5ft 8ins for a *chasseur*, with ten years' service, a good conduct record and a citation for valour. The Guard was increased in size by the formation of new regiments: the 2nd Grenadiers and 2nd Chasseurs, created on 15 April 1806, the Vélites having attained regimental strength by the formation of a second battalion in the previous November. The staff of the Grenadiers now stood at a colonel commandant, three majors (each commanding a regiment), six *chefs de bataillon*, six *adjutant-majors*, six *sous-adjutant-majors*, four *porte-drapeaux*, a drum-major, six *caporaux-tambours*, a *chef de musique* and 46 musicians; and each company was augmented by 20 *grenadiers*. (The six battalions described here were two each of the 1st and 2nd Grenadiers and two of the Vélite-Grenadiers.) On campaign it was usual for two Vélite companies to be attached to each Guard battalion, each company of which might comprise 80 Grenadiers and 45 Vélites.

For the Old Guard, Jena (1806) was as Austerlitz: they remained inactive as the army's reserve. The Vélites in particular couldn't conceal their impatience. Replied Napoleon to their cry of 'Forward!'—'Let a man wait until he has commanded in thirty pitched battles before he dares give me advice!' The Guard had more to do at Eylau, executing a bayonet charge, but was again inactive at Friedland; this, and the wretchedness of the winter of 1806–07, gave rise to a new nickname. They had previously been known as *sous-pieds de guêtre* (gaiter-straps), but now Napoleon coined for them a new sobriquet—*grognards* ('grumblers'). Their brief spell in the Iberian Peninsula again brought no general action, but caused more grumbling.

In an attempt to economise, in 1809 the two Grenadier regiments were amalgamated, and the Chasseurs likewise; the new corps had two battalions of four companies each, but with companies stronger than before. At Essling, where the Young Guard's baptism of fire cost it a quarter of its strength, Coignet recalled the bearskin caps of the Old Guard being flung 20 feet into the air when files were hit by roundshot. It was here that

Cantinière and Grenadier, in a Martinet print entitled '*Mde.d'Eau-de-vie suivent l'Armée*'. **The soldier wears a post-1808 cap. Note rolled** *bonnet de police* **below cartridge box; and grenade-shaped strap end attaching the box to the sabre belt. One hand-coloured copy of this print shows the Cantinière in a plain blue dress; black hat with pink band, over yellow headscarf with red zig-zags; brown cloak; grey-brown gaiters; red and white checkered neckerchief; and brown spirit flask on a tan strap.**

Napoleon, in unnecessary danger, was turned back by the Grenadiers' cry, 'lay down your arms unless the Emperor falls back!' At Wagram the Old Guard again served largely as a reserve, though 20 men from each company were detailed to replace gunners killed by Austrian fire; the 'Grumblers' were versatile!

On 13 September 1810 a new 2nd Regiment of Grenadiers was created, by the incorporation in the Imperial Guard of the ex-Royal Guard of the Kingdom of Holland when that state was absorbed into the Empire upon the abdication of Louis Bonaparte. In an Empire embracing many nationalities, there was little incongruity in the

Coat of the Colonel-Général of the Grenadiers à Pied, an appointment held by Davout—with cuff detail. The coat was of the usual colours, but with massive amounts of gold oakleaf embroidery; the gold epaulettes were worn on both shoulders, the gold aiguilettes on the right only. Epaulettes and buttons bore the crossed batons motif of a marshal; the coat was worn with a marshal's sash, and a fur cap with the white plume of a senior officer.

and without the extra pay and allowances granted to the 'old of the Old'.

All five regiments marched with Lefevre's 3rd Division of the Imperial Guard Corps in the Grande Armée for the invasion of Russia in 1812, the Chasseurs forming Boyer's Brigade and the Grenadiers Curial's Brigade. The Old Guard followed *Le Tondu* ('the clean-shaven one': their name for Napoleon), who slept amid their squares on the eve of Borodino; and they grumbled as ever when they were again left out of the battle. The Old Guard (strictly, only the 1st Regiments warranted that title, but the 2nd and Dutch regiments were included) actually increased in strength over the early part of the campaign—in contrast to the rest of the army—as more men came up from the rear. The returns show the following:

1st Chasseurs (Gen. Gros): *10 July* 33 officers, 1,359 men *10 October* 42 officers, 1,504 men

2nd Chasseurs (Col. Rosey): *10 July* 41 officers, 1,210 men *10 October* 40 officers, 1,324 men

1st Grenadiers (Col. Laurède): *10 July* 32 officers, 1,278 men *10 October* 39 officers, 1,346 men

2nd Grenadiers (Col. Harlet): *10 July* 34 officers, 1,030 men *10 October* 35 officers, 1,117 men

3rd Grenadiers (Gen. Tindal): *10 July* 38 officers, 1,074 men *10 October* 39 officers, 714 men—308 of the Dutch had 'disappeared' to the rear.

They accompanied the Emperor on the retreat, turning to rescue half the army at Krasny, where a battalion of the Dutch were decimated, the companies reduced to 20 men apiece. Throughout the horrors of the retreat from Moscow, the Old Guard was always there, always reliable, its discipline intact. The Westphalian Major Friedrich Wilhelm von Lossberg was told a story by an NCO of the Old Guard which illustrates the point. A French private, probably a Guardsman, began to rob the body of a dead officer to supplement his own meagre wardrobe, when the officer moaned, 'Friend, I am not yet dead!' The soldier stood to attention and said respectfully, 'Very well, sir! I'll wait a few moments longer.' The Guard was adept at looting; as Coignet said, when in the enemy's country, 'if you don't take anything, you feel you've forgotten something'. In Moscow the Grenadiers had even opened stalls to sell their booty, from jewellery to books, carriages to shoes—often the only way for the rest of the army to obtain its needs.

inclusion in the Guard of a 'foreign' regiment, whose colonel, Ralph Dundas Tindal, was Scottish! On 21 September 1810 the regiment was inaugurated officially as part of the Guard, comprising 46 officers, 1,188 NCOs and *grenadiers*, 16 *sapeurs*, 40 drummers and fifers and 153 *vélites*—the latter originally from Louis Bonaparte's Garde du Corps, the balance of which had gone straight into the Old Guard Grenadiers and Chasseurs. Recruiting to the Old Guard from men with ten years' service or distinguished conduct was becoming more difficult (in 1811 there were only 532 veterans of Italy and Egypt still serving in the Guard); but the ever-enlarging Guard had another new regiment formed on 18 May 1811, which ranked as the 2nd Grenadiers; the ex-Dutch regiment henceforth ranked as the 3rd Grenadiers. The 2nd Chasseurs was re-formed on the same day; and indeed it was said that the 2nd Grenadiers were superior in bearing even to the 1st, being 'younger, with better figures', if not quite in *esprit de corps*,

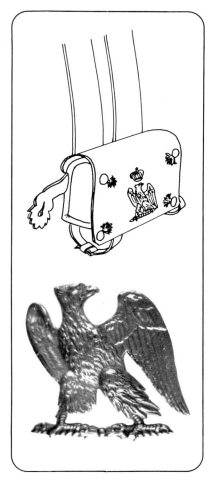

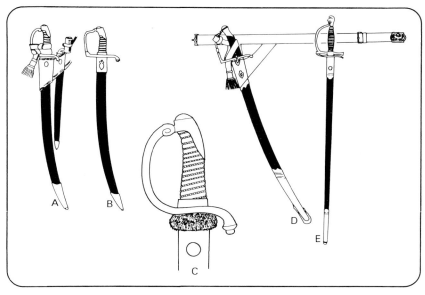

Grenadier cartridge box; and cast brass plate—the crown was a separate casting. The black leather box had brass flap devices, and white straps; the grenade-shaped one engaged with a button to stop the box slipping round the body, and the two below the box held the rolled *bonnet de police*.

(A) *Sabre-briquet* of Guard pattern, post-1802. (B) Sabre of Consular Guard pattern, pre-1802. (C) Hilt of the distinctive *sabre-briquet* used by the Old Guard. (D) Guard officer's sabre and waist belt. (E) Epée, as carried with undress uniform, and by musicians.

Even in the débâcle of retreat, they remained faithful; but the cost was unbearable. At Königsberg on Christmas Day, 1812, the Old Guard mustered:

1st Chasseurs:	28 officers,	435 men
2nd Chasseurs:	30 officers,	257 men
1st Grenadiers:	38 officers,	369 men
2nd Grenadiers:	39 officers,	234 men
3rd Grenadiers:	24 officers,	17 men

During the retreat, Bourgogne of the Guard Fusiliers met a man who asked him if he had noticed the Dutch Grenadiers pass. 'You didn't see it? That big sledge that overtook you contained the entire Dutch regiment! There were seven of them!' The Dutch regiment was disbanded on 15 February 1813. When the sick and injured were deducted, the Old Guard comprised 415 *chasseurs* and 408 *grenadiers* in February 1813; it was the beginning of the end.

Recruited up to strength again, the Grenadiers and Chasseurs formed the backbone of the expanded Guard which performed prodigies in 1813 and 1814, though the Young Guard bore the brunt and took the heaviest casualties. During a bombardment at Lützen, Napoleon exclaimed to the 2nd Chasseurs, 'What, does the Guard duck?' They stopped trying to take cover and were shot down accordingly. Though no longer filled with the 'old of the Old', throughout the campaigns of 1813–14 the Old Guard marched and fought with the same spirit. At Montmirail Gen. Henrion and his 2nd Chasseurs were ordered to charge a redoubt. They set off in column, under heavy fire; halted in square to repel a cavalry charge; reloaded, continued their advance, and captured the position. Shaking Henrion's hand, Napoleon remarked, 'General, I fully approve of your little halt during your charge!' As the sun of Empire sank, the 'Grumblers' remained the 'marching rampart' they had always been. When Paris fell, it was not before Lt. Viaux of the 2nd Grenadiers, convalescing there from his wounds, had gathered about 20 companions and attempted to defend Montmartre almost unaided. His body was found under a tree, sword in hand, surrounded by Prussian corpses.

As late as 3 April 1814 Napoleon still retained his Old Guard around him: 1,246 *chasseurs* and 50

Campaign uniform, 1806: print by R. Knötel based upon contemporary sources. (Left) *Sapeur*, Chasseurs. Scarlet-over-green plume; cap cords gold and green. *Surtout*; green epaulettes with scarlet crescent and fringe; green badge outlined gold; gold chevrons. Brass belt plate with horn device. (Centre) Grenadier. Usual colouring—though the Henschel original upon which this is based (from *Les Gardes Impériales et Royales de l'Armée Française*, Berlin) shows an even longer front tassel on the cap. (Right) Chasseur. Usual colouring—but Knötel exaggerates the red 'piping' on the collar shown by Henschel, which was in fact merely the inner lining of the *surtout*.

officers, and 1,287 *grenadiers* with 69 officers. Though the 'Grumblers' themselves cried that they should all go and 'end their careers in the ruins of the capital', further resistance was hopeless. After the formal abdication, a single battalion of Guardsmen was formed to accompany Napoleon to his new realm on Elba: 1,000 stalwarts, whose careers extended from Lodi to Acre, to Russia and back. For the rest, their service was transferred from the Imperial to the new Royal Guard, involving little more than a change of cockade; and, no doubt, a sublimation of true loyalties at the expense of earning their crust. The last act was played out at Fontainebleau, where Napoleon took a tearful farewell of his 'children', the Old Guard. His speech was not recorded *verbatim*, but it included a dramatic last gesture: 'I cannot embrace you all, but I shall embrace your general'—and, after Gen. Petit, he kissed the 'Eagle' of the 1st Grenadiers.

The Final Act

Under Louis XVIII the Old Guard consisted of the Royal Grenadiers and Royal Chasseurs, each regiment of three battalions, some 45 officers and 237 *grenadiers*, and 22 officers and 220 *chasseurs* were discharged on grounds of age or as incorrigible Bonapartists. When Napoleon returned to reclaim his throne at the beginning of the 'Hundred Days' the Guard returned to the Colours, in four regiments each of Grenadiers and Chasseurs; the 3rd Regts. were created on 8 April 1815 and the 4th Regts. on 9 May. But apart from the Elba Battalion and other *vieux moustaches* of the Royal Guard, it was not the Guard of old. The 1st Grenadiers (including the Elba men) were, as ever, the best, averaging 35 years of age, four-fifths of them holders of the *Légion d'Honneur*; the 2nd was also over 1,000 strong; but the 3rd, though it included some Elba veterans, was not well equipped, while the 4th had only 500 men and presented a motley appearance. The 1st and 2nd Chasseurs included some veteran officers and NCOs, but most had been Guardsmen only since 1813; the 3rd and 4th, the latter only one battalion strong, were costumed in even more random fashion. Among the 1st Grenadiers was the legendary *cantinière* Marie Tête-du-bois, known for her sharp tongue and warm heart, who had followed the regiment and ministered to it for many years, and to whom the Guard was her only home. Married to a drummer who was killed at Montmirail, she had borne him a son in the Marengo campaign; he too had become a drummer, and died in the defence of Paris.

In the Waterloo campaign the Old Guard was, as ever, held in reserve; but at the last it was committed when all else had failed, in an assault on the ridge of Mont St. Jean (though elements had been drawn off earlier in the day to reinforce the Young Guard in Plancenoit). Strangely, the exact sequence of the attack and even the battalions which took part in it are still matters for discussion, and there is much conflicting evidence. What is certain is that the battalions of Guardsmen who advanced up the slope ('as regularly formed as if at a field day' to quote Ensign Dirom of the British Foot Guards), accompanied by the crashing of drums and the hopes of France, represented Napoleon's last throw of the dice. Unable to break the Allied line, unwilling to retire, the 'bearskin bonnets' clung to the ridge with ranks convulsing like standing corn blown in the wind, as an eye-witness described poignantly, while they were swept by musketry and artillery fire. They almost succeeded; but in the end they broke. The cry 'La Garde recule' ('The Guard is thrown back') was the death-knell of the Empire. The 1st Grenadiers, 'oldest of the Old', still held in reserve, vainly tried to stem the flow of fugitives. Gen. Cambronne's alleged reply to the call to yield—'La Garde meurt et ne se rendent pas' ('The Guard dies but does not surrender')—was appropriate for many of the *vieux moustaches* who fell in the gloom of evening on 18 June 1815, even though his actual remark was probably simply '*Merde!*' Earlier in the day Marie Tête-du-bois had been killed by a roundshot; her sorrowing regiment erected a hastily-made wooden cross inscribed 'Here lies Maria, Cantinière of the 1st Grenadiers of the Old Imperial Guard, dead upon the field of honour 18 June 1815. Passerby, whoever you may be, salute Maria.'

The 1st Grenadiers marched away in formation, their drums beating the regimental call 'La Grenadière' to rally the shattered survivors of the other units. As Erckmann-Chatrian's character described, it 'sounded like an alarm-bell in the midst of a terrible fire . . . the last drum beat of France.' With Napoleon finally defeated and the Bourbons once more on the throne, the Guard was disbanded without delay: the 1st Grenadiers on 11 September, and the 2nd, 3rd and 4th on 24 September; the 3rd and 4th Chasseurs on 1 October, and the 1st and 2nd on the 11th. Some Guardsmen re-enlisted to serve the king; some travelled to the abortive French colony which was founded in Texas; more lived wretchedly on half-pay, watched suspiciously by the Bourbon police as they sat idly in the pavement cafés, re-living the past. When Napoleon's body returned to France in 1840 they paraded again, shrunken with age and wearing threadbare uniforms. The spirit, the ethos of the Old Guard was epitomised by *Grenadier Noisot*, who near Dijon erected at his own expense a magnificent bronze monument to the Emperor.

When he died he had himself buried in a standing position a few yards away, so that he could guard his Emperor through all eternity. By any standards, the Old Guard was unique.

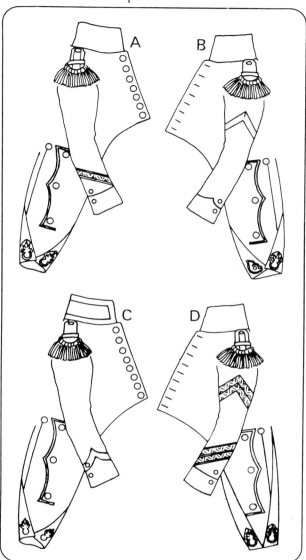

The *surtout*. (**A**) Sergeant, Grenadiers, of the style used before c.1806, with seven front buttons. Blue; scarlet lining, turnbacks and pocket piping; turnback badges as on the coat. Scarlet epaulettes with gold lace edging, crescent, *bride*, and a layer of gold fringe over the scarlet from 1806. Gold lace rank bar edged scarlet. (**B**) Chasseur, with the eight buttons worn c.1806–07. Colouring as above except for epaulettes of green with red fringe, *bride* and crescent (after 1805–06); orange service chevron. The Otto MS seems to err in showing nine to twelve buttons on the *surtout* in this period. (**C**) Apparent design worn by the Grenadier drummer in the Otto MS, except that we have reduced the number of front buttons here. Usual colouring with red epaulettes, gold lace round collar and, most unusually, pointed gold-laced cuffs. (**D**) Grenadier sergeant-major, of c.1811–15, with restyled turnbacks. Colouring as before ; gold epaulette edging, *bride*, top layer of fringe; gold rank bars edged scarlet; gold service chevrons.

The Regiments

1st Chasseurs Created as light infantry 2 December 1799; became Chasseurs à Pied 1801; disbanded 11 October 1815.

2nd Chasseurs Created 15 April 1806; amalgamated with 1st Regt. 1809. Re-formed 18 May 1811; disbanded 11 October 1815.

3rd Chasseurs Created 8 April 1815; disbanded 1 October 1815.

4th Chasseurs Created 9 May 1815; disbanded 1 October 1815.

1st Grenadiers Created 2 December 1799; disbanded 11 September 1815.

2nd Grenadiers Created 15 April 1806; amalgamated with 1st Regt. 1809. 2nd (Dutch) Regt. created from Royal Guard of Kingdom of Holland 13 September 1810, being re-numbered as 3rd Regt. on 18 May 1811 when a new 2nd (French) Regt. was created. This regiment was disbanded 24 September 1815.

3rd Grenadiers 2nd (Dutch) Regt. re-numbered as 3rd Regt. 18 May 1811; disbanded 15 February 1813. New 3rd (French) Regt. created 8 April 1815; disbanded 24 September 1815.

4th Grenadiers Created 9 May 1815; disbanded 24 September 1815.

Vélite-Grenadiers Created 29 July 1804.

Vélite-Chasseurs Created 29 July 1804.

Veterans. Compagnie des Vétérans created 12 July 1801; continued in existence under the Monarchy.

Uniforms

The Early Guards

The Grenadier-Gendarmes wore a uniform like the Gendarmerie Nationale but with a white piping on the collar, cuffs and lapels, and the traditional *grenadier* appointments of red epaulettes, fur cap and grenade-shaped turnback badges. The Garde de la

Grenadiers look on while Württemburg Jägers skirmish with Cossacks, 1812: print after Christian-Wilhelm von Faber du Faur. The trousers are rolled up, and the skirts of the greatcoats are gathered back off the legs for easy movement.

Convention wore a modified version of *gendarme* costume, originally with a hat but from 1795 with a fur cap with a red plume and a white-metal plate bearing a grenade and the legend (as on their buttons also) '*Grenadiers près la représentation nationale*'. The infantry-style dark blue (*bleu national*) coat had blue collar piped red, scarlet lapels and cuffs piped white, white cuff flaps piped scarlet, white metal buttons, horizontal pockets, white lining and turnbacks bearing red grenades, and red epaulettes; white waistcoat and breeches, with white gaiters in summer and black in winter. Their cartridge boxes bore circular plates emblazoned with a grenade and their title; they carried the infantry sabre and white leather equipment. Officers wore the same uniform with silver epaulettes, turnback grenades and sword knot, and a gorget. Later the cap plate bore the title '*Garde du Corps législatif*'.

The ill-discipline of the corps is demonstrated by a petition sent by them to the Directory, following an order that they should always appear in full dress: 'Well, what next? Is Liberty, then, to become an empty word? . . . Revoke, therefore, Citizens, revoke this order to be always in full dress. Are waistcoats and breeches to become an apple of discord thrown into Patriots' midst to divide them and strengthen the Royalists? Not in the accoutrements, but in the heart, lies the sanctuary of Republicanism . . .'—a convenient excuse to avoid wearing the more uncomfortable items of uniform!

The Garde du Directoire wore a uniform like that of infantry *grenadiers*: fur cap with brass plate bearing a grenade and '*Garde du Directoire exécutif*', with a red and blue rear patch bearing a white lace cross, a red plume and red cords; dark blue coat with scarlet collar and cuffs, white lapels, cuff flaps and turnbacks, red horizontal pocket-piping, red grenade turnback-badge, and brass buttons bearing a lictor's fasces and the motto as on the cap plate; red epaulettes and sword knot; with waistcoat, breeches, gaiters and equipment like the infantry. Officers had gold distinctions, their waist belt a gilt plate bearing the letters 'R.F.' (*République Française*). This uniform was basically that retained by the Consular Guard until 1801, with only a change in button design, and was probably that worn in the 1800 campaign.

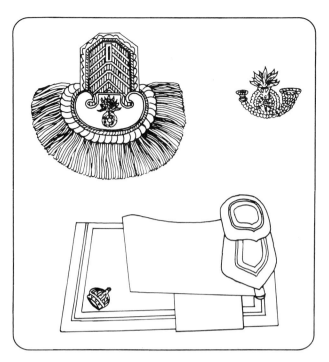

(**Top left**) **Officer's epaulette, Grenadiers à Pied:** gold lace on red cloth backing, with the gold fringe worn by junior officers—those above the rank of captain had bullion fringes. (**Top right**) The gold embroidered and sequinned grenade-and-horn device which replaced the simple grenade on the straps of Chasseur officers' epaulettes. (**Bottom**) **Officer's horse furniture.** This usually consisted of dark blue cloth shabraque and holster caps with gold lace decoration, including a gold crown in the rear corners; the badge may conceivably have been replaced on occasion by a gold grenade or horn. Colonels-general of the Grenadiers and Chasseurs holding the rank of marshal would have the same design but in crimson, with an additional gold fringe edging.

Grenadiers à Pied

Orders of Dress

After a decree of 21 Fructidor Year VIII (8 September 1800) which established the Guard's organisation, a list of equipment for each man was prepared: two coats, two waistcoats, two pairs of breeches, forage cap, pair of shoes, pair of black gaiters, pair of white gaiters, hat with pompon, cockade and end-tassels, pair of hose, buckles for stock, gaiters and shoes, hide knapsack, bearskin cap with plate, cords and plume, cartridge box with grenade plate, belts with stitched edges, sword knot, and fatigue smock. The total cost was 258 francs per man. (Guard uniforms were always a considerable expense; between 1807 and 1810 alone they cost the treasury over 20 million francs.) The basic 'orders of dress' worn by the Grenadiers were as follows:

Parade dress (*Tenue de grande parade*) Coat, fur cap

Grenadier, c.1813, wearing the classic campaign uniform of the Old Guard in the latter years of the Empire: a cap bare of cords and plume; the greatcoat, here with the two service chevrons indicating between 15 and 20 years' service; blue trousers worn over gaiters, in this case white; and equipment including a cloth cartridge box cover, visible on the background figures. The old Grenadier wears his *Légion d'Honneur* **on the left breast.**

with ornaments, white waistcoat and breeches, white stock, white gaiters with white buttons.

Ordinary full dress (Grande tenue habituelle) As above, but black stock and black gaiters with brass buttons.

Winter walking-out dress (Tenue de sortie d'hiver) Coat or *surtout*, white waistcoat, blue breeches tucked into 'Suvarov' boots (similar to unlaced 'Hessians'), hat, sabre suspended from a single shoulder belt; in cold weather the greatcoat could replace the coat, with blue trousers worn over black gaiters.

Summer walking-out dress (Tenue de sortie d'été) Coat or *surtout*, twilled cloth waistcoat, hat, breeches of cotton, twilled cloth or nankeen (sometimes pale

chamois in colour), white stockings, silver-buckled shoes.

Marching order or campaign dress (Tenue de route ou de campagne) Coat or *surtout*, waistcoat, blue or white trousers over grey gaiters with horn buttons, hat; fur bonnet carried on knapsack. After 1809, hats carried on knapsack and bonnet worn with waterproof cover. For example, an order of the day of 2 Prairial Year XIII (22 May 1804) notes that 'on the march, *grenadiers* should wear the *surtout*, waistcoat and breeches, linen trousers, grey gaiters and hat. In the knapsack, bonnet in cover, plume, linen smock, two pairs of shoes, black cloth gaiters, white cotton gaiters, waistcoat and breeches, black and white stock, two shirts and forage cap. Black stock worn on the march. Full dress uniforms to be packed onto transport waggons.' Full dress was usually donned immediately before an action, to render the Old Guard as imposing a sight as possible—as before Borodino, when Heinrich von Brandt of the Vistula Legion described them as standing out from the rest by virtue of wearing 'their parade uniforms, with their red plumes and epaulettes showing across the fields like a stripe of blood'.

Fatigue dress (Tenue de corvée) Forage cap (*bonnet de police*), loose white linen smock (*sarreau*) buttoned at neck and wrist; white linen or blue cloth trousers.

The Grenadier Cap (Bonnet à poil)

Colloquially known as the 'beehive', the traditional fur grenadier cap was the most distinctive feature of Old Guard uniform. The Consular Guard version was made of black bearskin with a scarlet rear patch bearing an orange lace cross. (Note: the term 'orange', used here for convenience, usually applies to the colour *aurore* for which no adequate translation exists; usually it had a golden tint.) Its brass plate bore an embossed grenade, of which several varieties existed, the plate having either 'straight' or 'wavy' sides. From about 1800–01 the original plate was replaced by a slightly smaller version, of stamped brass bearing a grenade over a scroll reading '*Garde des Consuls*', all within a laurel wreath, as shown by Alexis Chataignier; See Plate A1. The wavy-sided plate had an oak-leaf edging, though Hoffman shows another variety with the scroll above the grenade. Originally the cap had scarlet woollen braided cords suspended around it

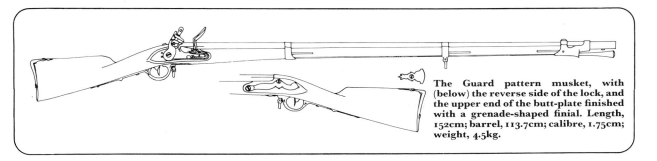

The Guard pattern musket, with (below) the reverse side of the lock, and the upper end of the butt-plate finished with a grenade-shaped finial. Length, 152cm; barrel, 113.7cm; calibre, 1.75cm; weight, 4.5kg.

(from top right to bottom left), ending in a single oval *raquette*, with a red plume above a tricolour cockade at the left side. At the same time as the adoption of the new plate the cords became white, and in July 1802 (according to Fallou) the lace cross on the rear patch also became white.

The Old Guard 'beehive' was larger than often depicted, measuring 33cm high at the front, increased to 35cm by the thickness of fur. The white tassel hanging at the front from the crown was attached permanently; Martinet in 1808 and Genty in 1815 show two tassels, as more usually seen on the caps of the Chasseurs. A new plate was introduced with the advent of the Empire, bearing a crowned eagle flanked by grenades. This was first issued in October 1804, though the exact date of change is uncertain. At the end of 1805 some 2,033 of the new plates were in store, perhaps suggesting the retention of the Consular Guard plates for some months, or even the existence of an intermediate pattern—perhaps represented by an extant plate bearing an uncrowned eagle, flanked by grenades, with an engraved cockade at the top. The crowned-eagle plate was initially of stamped brass, but was later struck in copper.

The white plaited cords (costing 3 F.50) ended in oval *raquettes*, contemporary pictures and surviving examples showing both one and two *raquettes*; conceivably one regiment or battalion adopted a second as a distinctive device, though as the price of the cord does not seem to have altered the latter may have been of inferior quality (?). In 1808 the white cross on the rear patch was replaced by an embroidered white grenade. The cockade at the base of the scarlet plume was always of tricolour design (white edge, red inner, blue centre); originally it was of pleated lace, and after 1806 the wide blue centre bore a crowned eagle embroidered in orange wool. From about 1806–08 the cockade

was made like a hemispherical half-pompon, in wool; after 1811 it reverted to pleated lace.

Barrès of the Chasseurs notes that prior to departure for Italy in 1805, the bonnets were carried on the march in 'cardboard cases like a lady's muff-box', which collapsed into pulp with the first shower of rain, letting the bonnets fall into the mud; 'imagine soldiers having to carry such hideous things in their hands or under their arms! We looked a regular band of gipsies.' Immediately afterwards (Barrès says 17 January 1805) bags of blue and white striped ticking were provided, in which the caps were stowed, to be attached to the knapsack. 'We were advised to obtain straps, without any particular length or colour being specified, so that there was a regular medley.' The cardboard boxes were presumably a temporary measure until the bags could be distributed. Latterly, the bearskin bonnets were worn on campaign with cords and plume removed and with a black waterproof cover (e.g. as shown by Albrecht Adam's sketches of the retreat from Moscow), the plume in an oilskin tube often being carried strapped to the sabre scabbard. The caps could deteriorate on campaign even without accidents like that which befell Barrès, when during the 1805 campaign half his cap was eaten by a goat.

The Hat (Chapeau)

The bicorn hat worn in walking-out dress and on the march differed from the infantry type in having orange wool 'ties' on front and back and V-shaped cockade loop; red *marrons* or *floches* at the ends (terminals or 'tassels', not always fringed); and a red carrot-shaped plume, worn by the Consular Guard. In 1800 the hat cost 8 F.75, was made of black felt, and bore the tricolour cockade; in 1804 it cost 12 F., but a year later was reduced to 10 F.75. A new pattern was adopted in 1811, wider than the

Sapeur, **Grenadiers, c.1810: a Pierre Martinet print. Cap with white cords (note two frontal tassels), scarlet plume. Scarlet epaulettes with gold (?) transverse *bride*; white axes badge outlined red; brass belt plate; eagle-headed sabre; brass lion masks on crossbelts. Note apron worn over the waistcoat but under the coat; on campaign (as Adam shows) it could be worn over the greatcoat.**

preceding type and edged with black braid, bearing an increased number of 'ties', and costing 12 F. Both patterns bore the carrot-shaped pompon, shown by some sources as topped by a red tuft. The hat was never popular on campaign, the bonnet being preserved for special occasions; Barrès records the Guard throwing away their hats, which were 'in such bad condition' on 14 June 1807, en route to Friedland, 'amidst cries of joy from the whole of the Guard'; but hats were re-issued in the last weeks of 1807. The hat was finally rejected as ordinary campaign dress on 21 May 1809, while the Guard was actually on the march; each man unpacked from the knapsack the fur cap of the man in front, and hurled his bicorn hat into the Danube! When not worn on campaign, the hats were carried in the ticking bag which had contained the bonnet.

Hairstyles

Uniquely in the French army, the Old Guard retained the powdered queue of the 18th century, which they were supposed to dress every day, even on campaign. Coignet described the hairstyle as 'brushed out in front like pigeon's wings', with a six-inch queue tied by a black worsted ribbon with two-inch ends and pinned with a silver grenade. 'Sideboards' were worn to the depth of the ear-lobe; and from 1 March to 1 December each year moustaches were worn, being shaved off during winter until 1806–07, after which moustaches were worn at all times. Gold earrings were virtually an item of uniform, each new recruit having his ears pierced, and according to Capt. Hippolyte de Mauduit it was common to wear tattoos on arms or chest, depicting grenades or eagles, etc.

The Coat (Habit)

The uniform of the Garde du Directoire seems to have been kept by the Consular Guard until 1800–01, including the scarlet collar and white turnbacks, with only a change to buttons bearing the lictor's fasces and legend '*Garde des Consuls*' and '*Rep. Franc.*' The specifications of 8 September 1800 describe a new coat, of blue cloth with blue collar, white lapels and three-pointed cuff flaps; scarlet cuffs, piping to vertical pockets, lining and turnbacks, with ornaments of orange grenades upon white cloth backing; 22 large and 11 small buttons; and epaulettes with transverse strap, the latter stitched permanently to the coat, of scarlet with white piping and lining.

This pattern of coat remained basically unchanged throughout the Empire (the Old Guard never adopted the *habit-veste* of 1812), but with a gradual alteration of cut. The lapels, each bearing seven buttons, were gradually given a more accentuated curve, revealing more of the waistcoat; Barrès dated one re-modelling to the last weeks of 1807, claiming the new style was an improvement copied from the Russians. The skirts were both shortened and narrowed; under the Consulate they extended to the knee, but by 1810 barely reached the top of the gaiters. From about 1808 the turnbacks were stitched down to the skirts, and around 1810 were made to extend to the bottom edge of the coat, eliminating the small blue triangle previously visible at the bottom. New 'Imperial' buttons, bearing a crowned eagle but no motto, were apparently distributed in October–November 1804, but first noted on 9 November. Originally brass, the buttons were replaced by copper in 1811. Pocket design (vertical, piped scarlet and each with three buttons) remained unchanged, as did the three buttons positioned below the right-hand lapel. After 1809 the epaulette fringes became slightly longer and thicker. The exact shade of dark blue probably varied slightly after c.1808, due to the shortage of indigo dye; plants grown within the Empire, principally woad, were used thereafter. Both the coat and *surtout* were lined with scarlet, probably explaining the apparent red 'piping' visible in some pictures, merely the result of the lining of old garments having stretched sufficiently to be visible.

Sapeur, **Grenadiers, full dress, c.1810: print by E. Giffard from the Bucquoy series. This shows the full dress introduced in about that year, with red-and-gold lace on the facings and seams, and epaulettes and cap cords of the same mixture.** *Sapeurs* **wore gold grenades on the turnbacks; in undress, their plain** *surtouts* **had gold lace round the cuffs, and their sabre was slung from a single shoulder belt.**

The Surtout

The single-breasted *surtout* came into service in 1802, replacing the issue of one of the two coats. Blue throughout, it had plain round cuffs which opened at the rear with two small buttons; the front was fastened by a row of seven large buttons. Epaulettes, pockets and turnbacks were coloured as for the coat. It was worn on the march, in undress and in the field; the Guard wore it in the campaigns of 1806 and 1807. The short front became slightly longer, having eight buttons in 1806 and nine after 1807; although retained for senior NCOs, *grenadiers* and corporals seem to have lost it after 1810.

Waistcoat and legwear

The single-breasted white waistcoat was sleeved and had a standing collar, with twelve small brass buttons at the front and two at each cuff; it became slightly shorter at the time the lapels of the coat received their accentuated curve. It could be worn instead of the coat in hot climates, with epaulettes attached (as in Spain), or instead of the smock for fatigues. A white stock was reserved for those occasions when white gaiters were worn; otherwise black stocks were used, though Coignet mentions a 'double cravat', white on one side and black with a narrow white edge on the other. Prior to 1801 the

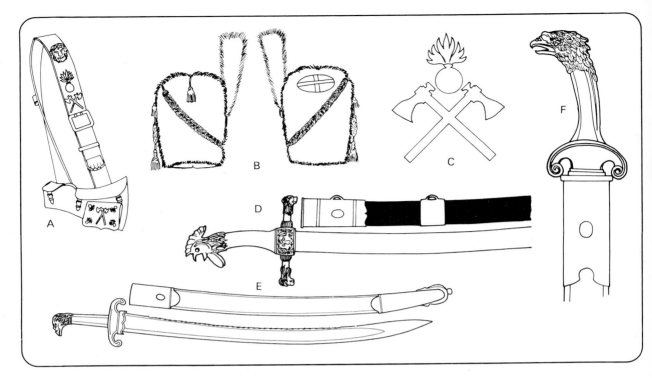

(**A**) *Sapeur's* **axe case and belt: white leather belt, black leather case with small black leather pouch attached, both with gilded fittings, buckles and badges. The haft of the axe fitted through the leather loop on the rear of the belt. (B)** *Sapeur's* **cap, Grenadiers à Pied, with the rear patch worn before 1808 and the 'flat' cockade worn before c.1806–08. (C)** *Sapeur's* **sleeve badge, variously depicted in contemporary sources: sometimes with a second grenade below, sometimes with axes alone, in various colours—usually gold, or gold on red backing. (The badge is white on the enigmatic red uniform of the Dutch Grenadiers'** *tête de colonne*.) **Hoffman shows a** *sapeur* **without any badges. More elaborate-seeming versions are no more than the usual badge superimposed upon the ordinary service chevron on the left sleeve. (D) Early pattern sabre used by Guard** *sapeurs*: **the gilded brass hilt has a cockerel-head pommel, rams'-head quillons and a lion mask on the quillon block. (E) Guard** *sapeur's* **sabre with eagle-head pommel and saw-toothed back. (F) Alternative Guard** *sapeur* **sabre hilt pattern.**

Consular Guard wore white breeches and white or black gaiters according to season; in 1802 there appeared new summer waistcoats and breeches in cotton. The original white linen gaiters (extending over the knee) were replaced for parade by gaiters of twilled cloth (*basin*) with white buttons; black gaiters with brass buttons were reserved for ordinary full dress, with the grey linen with horn buttons used for marching order and field dress from 1803–04. In October 1805 Hulin issued an order to the effect that 'The Commandant has noticed several soldiers wearing black gaiters on the march and reminds them of the regulations expressly ordering them to wear grey'; but on campaign many other styles were used. These included wide blue trousers (*pantalons de route*) worn above the gaiters, adopted upon Dorsenne's orders in November 1805, and remaining in use until 1815. Other recorded colours of trousers include the usual

Grenadier *tête de colonne* **in full dress: left to right—drummer, musician, drum-major, cymbalist,** *sapeurs*. **The drum-major wears a heavily laced uniform, but the** *sapeur* **does not have lace on his coat seams, and the musician has lapel loops without tassels, perhaps suggesting a date of c.1810 (although the print is not contemporary). The cymbalist wears the uniform of turban and** *surtout* **shown by Chataignier.**

grey, white or beige, and blue-and-white ticking; Albrecht Adam shows trousers tucked into knee-length gaiters in 1812. An (unofficial) optional extra for wear with the breeches, stockings and silver garter-buckles for walking-out dress were false calves, as adopted by Coignet to disguise his spindly legs; they cost him 18 francs, but when 'entertained' by a society lady he was in a torment about how to disguise them, eventually stowing them under the pillow of her bed and pulling them on (crookedly) under the bedclothes in the morning! Barrès noted that in 1805 his shoes were flat-soled and extremely unstable in open country, while Coignet had to tie his on with string around the ankles to avoid losing them in the mud in 1806.

Greatcoats

An official issue of greatcoats was ordered first on 30 November 1804 and distributed in the following month. An extant example is blue, double-breasted with two rows of eight large buttons, with four at the rear of the waist and on the pockets, and two small buttons on each cuff. The straps to secure the epaulettes were red, edged white. A grenadier in the Boersch collection (Plate D3), dated perhaps 1807 but possibly as late as 1813, wears a coat with red

(Left) Drum-major: print by Pierre Martinet. Although identified only as 'Garde Impériale: Tambour Major', it obviously represents the Grenadiers' drum-major. Note the amount of gold lace on the coat seams and breeches: such a uniform might cost as much as 30,000 francs.

(Centre) Drum-major of the Grenadiers in campaign dress: print from Costumes des corps de l'armée française avant et pendant le Révolution, **by Charlet. This well-known print shows the** petit tenue: **basically an ordinary coat with gold lace on collar and cuffs only, gold rank bars and epaulettes, and gold 'ties' on the hat. The high boots are unusual—in later years long trousers were probably more common. Though he retains his mace, his baldric has been discarded.**

(Right) Grenadier drummer, full dress, c.1810: print after P. A. Leroux from the Bucquoy series. This shows the full dress after removal of the 'wings', with mixed red-and-gold lace on the facings—including brandenbourgs **on the lapels—and red-and-gold epaulettes. On campaign lace was restricted to a single line around the collar and cuffs. Brass drum with light blue hoops, both bearing brass grenade badges.**

cuff-piping and a red collar patch piped white and bearing a button. These were not uncommon additions to greatcoats, and are known to have been used by the Chasseurs (q.v.). Sky-blue coats taken into use in 1811 were withdrawn after a short time on Napoleon's orders.

Forage cap (Bonnet de police)

Of the type known as 'à la dragonne', the blue cloth forage cap had orange lace, an orange tassel-end and an orange grenade on the front; from 1802 the 'wing' of the cap was piped with orange braid. It was usually carried rolled beneath the cartridge box, secured by two leather straps.

Equipment

The equipment was basically of infantry style, though the white leather belts and musket sling usually had stitched edges. The black, waxed leather cartridge box originally bore a brass grenade badge, replaced in 1804 (probably for the Coronation) by a crown over an eagle, with a small grenade in each corner, initially brass but later copper; the white leather strap which secured it in place was shaped at the end like a grenade, and fastened to a leather button on the other belt. A cover for use on campaign was in service in 1805, probably of white linen with the eagle and grenades stencilled in black; Fallou mentions a cover of black, waxed linen with orange devices, but the source is unrecorded. The sabre, of special Guard pattern with brass hilt, black leather grip and black scabbard with brass fittings, was issued in 1802, replacing the earlier Consular Guard sabre which had a more angular guard. The original red sword knot was replaced by one with a white leather strap and red tassel c.1802–03.

The calfskin knapsack was closed by three leather straps, with two upper straps added later to secure the rolled greatcoat, and later a longer strap to encircle both coat and knapsack. Equipment lists of 1811 mention 'havresac, grand modèle', as different from the smaller knapsacks used by the Line. Campaign equipment included a canteen of some description (flask, bottle in wicker case, or gourd) suspended on a cord and sanctioned by an order of 13 September 1806, and camp equipment such as white-metal cooking pots (marmites) or messtins (gamelles) in fabric covers, plus personal impedimenta such as the collection of literature prized by Lt. Faré as his most important possessions.

NCOs

Rank markings were in the form of diagonal bars worn above the cuff:

Corporal: (not officially 'NCOs', the term being limited to sergeants and above): two orange wool bars, edged red.
Sergeant: Gold bar edged red on each sleeve; epaulette straps edged with gold lace, with gold 'crescent', gold transverse strap edged red and, after 1806, a layer of gold fringe atop the red. Epaulettes cost 9 F. per pair in 1804, 16 F. in 1806 and 20 F. in 1811. Mixed red and gold cap-cords, sword knot, hat terminals and 'ties', gold cockade loop, gilt buttons; carried an épée in walking-out dress suspended from a waist belt passing behind the breeches-flap.
Fourrier: Gold diagonal bar on upper arm, sergeants' epaulettes, corporals' rank bars.
Sergeant-major: Two gold rank bars, gold-laced epaulettes and crescents, layer of gold fringe over the red, and two layers after 1806. Epaulettes cost 14 F. in 1803, 26 F. in 1806 and 30 F. in 1810.
Service chevrons: Inverted V-shaped chevrons worn on left upper arm, one for ten years' service, two for 15 to 20, and three for 20 to 25. Orange lace for grenadiers and corporals, gold lace for others.

Officers

Officers' uniforms followed those of the rank-and-file, but in finer material. Gold cap cords and patch-decoration, Hoffman c.1804 showing the use of double cords, one length plain and one plaited; colonels and majors had white plumes to their bearskins. Officers' coats had gilt buttons and gold turnback badges, and gold lace epaulettes with rank distinction as follows:

Colonel: Both epaulettes fringed with bullion.
Major: As colonel, but silver straps.
Chef de bataillon: Bullion fringe on left epaulette only.
Captain: Cord fringe (not bullion) on left epaulette only.
Lieutenant: As captain, but a silk line on the epaulette.
Sous-lieutenant (second lieutenant): As lieutenant, but two red silk lines on the strap.
Capt.-Adjutant-Major: Fringe on right epaulette only.

The straps bore a chevron-pattern lace upon red backing, bearing an embroidered grenade in relief; the fringe became slightly longer and thicker after 1809. The gilt gorgets bore silver eagles within oak and laurel sprays, and the waist belt plates were rectangular, bearing initially a gilt grenade and edging upon silver, or all gilt as shown by Potrelle; and later an eagle within an oak spray, either gilt or in silver on gilt. The waist belt (of white, or occasionally black leather as shown by the Otto MS) supported a sabre in a leather frog, with black

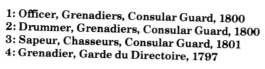

1: Officer, Grenadiers, Consular Guard, 1800
2: Drummer, Grenadiers, Consular Guard, 1800
3: Sapeur, Chasseurs, Consular Guard, 1801
4: Grenadier, Garde du Directoire, 1797

A

1: Officer, Grenadiers, full dress, 1805
2: Vélite, full dress, 1805
3: Sergeant-major, Grenadiers, walking-out, 1805

B

1: Drum-major, Grenadiers, 1804
2: Cymbalist, Grenadiers, 1804
3: Musician, Chasseurs, 1808

1: Chasseur, campaign dress, 1807
2: Officer, Grenadiers, marching order, 1807
3: Grenadier, campaign dress, 1807
4: Grenadier, campaign dress, 1807

D

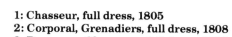

1: Chasseur, full dress, 1805
2: Corporal, Grenadiers, full dress, 1808
3: Drummer, Chasseurs, full dress, 1808
4: Grenadier in fatigue smock, 1808

E

1: Sergeant, Chasseurs, full dress, 1810
2: Lieutenant Porte-Aigle, 1st Grenadiers, 1811
3: Sapeur, Grenadiers, full dress, 1810

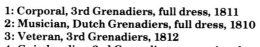

1: Corporal, 3rd Grenadiers, full dress, 1811
2: Musician, Dutch Grenadiers, full dress, 1810
3: Veteran, 3rd Grenadiers, 1812
4: Guimbardier, 3rd Grenadiers, campaign dress, 1812

G

1: Sergeant, Grenadiers, campaign dress, 1812-15
2: Officer, Grenadiers, campaign dress, 1812-15
3: Sergeant-major, Chasseurs, undress, 1812-15
4: Chasseur, marching order, 1815

scabbard, gilded fittings and gold knot. The *surtout* and bicorn hat were worn frequently on campaign (the hat with gold loop, 'ties' and tassel-ends), and legwear included white breeches worn with tan-topped boots, or riding boots for mounted officers, and blue breeches or long trousers on campaign. *Porte-Aigles* wore white gaiters on parade, and the earlier *Porte-Drapeaux* are shown with black gauntlets. Mounted officers' square-cut blue shabraques had gold lace edging and crown badges in the rear corners, with matching holster covers.

Sapeurs

In common with *sapeurs* (pioneers) of infantry, those of the Guard wore fur caps without plates, full beards, white leather aprons and carried axes and carbines; their 'orders of dress' were like those of the other ranks, the *surtout* and bicorn being worn when appropriate. The *sapeurs* wore gold and red cap-cords, sergeants' epaulettes and sword knots, and gold crossed axes badges on red upon the upper sleeves—though a number of varieties of epaulette and badge design are recorded, as detailed under plate F3. Hoffman shows the use in full dress (c.1804) of mixed red and gold lace on the collar, lapels (including tassel-ended loops or *brandenbourgs*), cuffs, flaps and turnbacks, though it was apparently not until around April 1810 that the *sapeurs* received a coat with the additional red and gold lace on the facings, pockets and sleeve-seams and *brandenbourgs* to each button, as shown in Plate F3. The *surtout* had gold lace on collar and cuffs and was worn with a sergeant's hat. Their shoulder belts are shown ornamented with various gilt badges, buckles, sliders and tips, including simple crossed axes, grenades, a lion-mask over axes on red cloth backing with or without a grenade between, or a lion-mask alone (Martinet). Otto shows a pouch worn at the front of the waist belt, bearing badges like a cartridge box; other sources show a rectangular belt plate bearing a grenade, supporting a distinctive sabre with guardless brass hilt in the shape of a cockerel-head, or later an eagle-head; their axe cases were black leather with a small cartridge box attached, bearing gilt crossed axes and corner grenades.

Drummers

Drummers wore the basic uniform of the grena-diers, with distinctive features. The Consular Guard had gold-laced collars and lapels, including *brandenbourgs*, and scarlet epaulettes over gold-laced wings (apparently shown blue by Potrelle), or with orange lace instead. Later full dress distinctions included scarlet 'swallows'-nest' style wings edged gold under the epaulettes, discontinued in 1808, and mixed red and gold lace on the collar, lapels (including *brandenbourgs*), cuffs, flaps, pockets and turnbacks; the epaulettes were red and gold with mixed fringe. For ordinary dress, their uniforms were distinguished only by gold lace edging the collar and cuffs, the latter shown (perplexingly) as pointed on the *surtout* in the Otto MS of 1807–08. Their drum-belts bore brass grenade badges over the drumstick holder; the brass drums, sometimes shown with embossed grenades, are shown with hoops of light blue (Potrelle, Consular Guard), triangles of red or blue alternating with white on the outer edges (Otto), or blue with brass grenades. The uniform of the drum-majors was amongst the most magnificent of the era, as shown by Hoffman, upon which Plate C1 is based; the vast expense of this uniform for the Consular Guard included plumes at 195 F., baldric at 1,250 F., and sabre and belt at 1,460 francs. Even the plainer uniform worn on campaign included gold-laced collar and cuffs, gold epaulettes and two gold rank bars, an officers' sabre suspended from gold-laced scarlet baldric with gilt grenade over the drumstick holder, and a gold-laced hat with red plume. A similar uniform had been worn by the drum-major of the Garde du Directoire, with a red-over-white-over-blue plume.

Musicians

The band of the Garde du Directoire wore ordinary uniform but with scarlet 'stand-and-fall' collar and 'gauntlet' cuffs edged gold, and a gold-laced bicorn. Potrelle shows the musicians of the Consular Guard with gold-laced bicorn with crimson and white feather edging and red or red-tipped white plume; blue coat with crimson facings laced gold, including gold *brandenbourgs* on the crimson lapels and gold trefoil epaulettes, though the former are absent from the fifers' uniform; waistcoat and legwear as for *grenadiers*, but an épée with red knot suspended from a waist belt which has a gilt rectangular plate bearing a grenade. Hoffman shows the uniform of c.1804 including a gold-laced hat with edging of

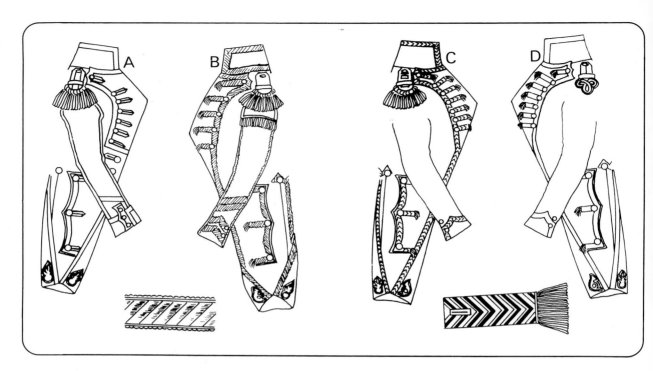

(A) Apparent coat design worn by Tambour-Maître, Grenadiers à Pied, after the '*Collections Alsaciennes*': blue, with scarlet cuffs, turnbacks, lining and pocket piping; white lapels and cuff flaps. Gold lace on facings, including pointed-end loops and sleeve seams; scarlet epaulettes with gold crescents. Worn with gold-edged bicorn with gold 'ties' and scarlet plume. (B) Drum-major, Chasseurs à Pied, after the print published by Jean in 1803: colouring as before, but additional gold lace of interwoven diagonal design with scalloped edges; *brandenbourgs* with gold fringes. Gold bullion epaulettes are worn on top of scarlet 'swallows'-nest' wings, which have gold piping and gold bullion fringe. (Below) Design of B's lace. (C) Drummer, Chasseurs, 1808. Blue with scarlet lining, turnbacks, cuffs and pocket piping; white lapels; gold lace with interwoven green chevron pattern. Green epaulettes laced gold, green crescent, gold fringe overlaid on green, gold *bride* on scarlet. (D) Musician, Chasseurs, 1808. Blue with crimson lining, turnbacks, cuffs and pocket piping; gold lace; gold trefoils on crimson backing. Prior to this date it seems that only five *brandenbourgs* were worn on the lapels. (Below) *Brandenbourg* of C's lace.

red/light blue/white feathers and white-over-red plume; blue coat with crimson facings and gold lace as before; but a gold sword knot, plain gilt waist belt plate, and a brass horn with cords and two tassels of mixed gold, blue and red. By c.1805 the hat edging had become red and white, with white plume, and officers' boots were worn in all but parade dress; in 1810 the plume was given a red base, the gold 'ties' on the hat were discontinued, scarlet replaced crimson as the facing colour and pointed-ended lapel-loops seem to have been adopted, and 'Suvarov' boots replaced the tan-topped variety. It seems possible that the *brandenbourgs* may have been removed at the same time as the re-styling of the

turnbacks. In undress (*petit uniforme*) a *surtout* like that of the *grenadiers* was worn, with gold lace upon the collar, cuffs, and red turnbacks, with gold trefoils, plain hat, red plume, and blue breeches in winter; after about 1809 an ordinary *habit* was worn in undress with gold lace only upon the collar, cuffs and turnbacks. Negro percussionists wore the uniform shown in Plate C2, though a Chataignier illustration of c.1801 shows a cymbalist with a crimson turban with white pagri and gilt chains hanging from the top of the cap, a white *aigrette* at the left and two gold tassels; blue *surtout* with crimson lining and collar, gold epaulettes and collar lace and *brandenbourgs* on the breast; crimson waistcoat and breeches with gold lace and Austrian knots; gold-laced hussar boots, white waist belt with gilt plate bearing a grenade, and épée with gold knot. Much the same costume is shown as late as 1805–10.

The Restoration

The Bourbon Restoration merely obliterated the Imperial symbols on the uniform; the arms of the monarchy now appeared upon the cap plate and cartridge box, and a crowned fleur-de-lys on the buttons. Upon the return from Elba the royal arms were removed from the cap plate, a tricolour cockade filling the gap; but soon after new plates, cartridge box eagles, and buttons were distributed. Charlet shows Royal Grenadiers with a cartridge box cover bearing the usual black grenades, plus a large black grenade in the centre, and Dighton depicts similar ornaments in brass. During the 'Hundred Days' it was reported that the 3rd Grenadiers had insufficient bonnets, wearing shakos, hats and forage caps instead, with some musket slings replaced by string; while the 4th were so short of equipment as to resemble provincial national guards. It is recorded that 32 new dress uniforms for the band turned up in November 1815, and were worn ultimately by the new *Garde Royale*.

infantry style lapels with pointed lower ends, and scarlet pointed cuffs piped white; the orange turnback badges on white patches consisted of a hunting horn on the front turnbacks and a grenade on the rear. The epaulettes, originally green with blue lining and red crescents, from 1805–06 had red fringes and transverse straps and a second red crescent inside the first; though the Otto MS shows green straps and crescent and red fringe.

The *surtout* had pointed cuffs, and the forage cap an orange hunting-horn in front. Legwear and waistcoats were as for the Grenadiers, but long trousers are mentioned in inventories as early as

Chasseurs à Pied

The Chasseurs of the Consular Guard are the first light unit whose uniform is known; that of the original light infantry company is unknown. Their equipment was described as like that of the Grenadiers, save for a lack of cap plates and with hunting-horn cartridge box badges. Listed in a Consular Guard inventory of 1800 are items later worn by the Chasseurs: green epaulettes and sword knots, bonnets and plumes, and NCOs' epaulettes, cap cords and hat ornaments of green-and-gold. In many aspects the uniform of the Chasseurs à Pied of the Imperial Guard was like that of the Grenadiers, but with the differences noted below.

The Chasseurs' fur bonnet never had a plate, but originally *may* have included a rear patch like that of the Grenadiers; it is shown as late as the Otto MS, but was probably never seen after 1806, though evidence is unclear. The white cords were like those of the Grenadiers, apparently always with two *raquettes*, and two hanging tassels at the front (Otto shows one). The plume was always green with a red tip; during the Consular period the green was two-thirds the height, extending above the top of the bonnet, in 1806 the proportions were reversed so that the green scarcely reached the top of the cap. The hat resembled that of the Grenadiers save for green *marrons* at the ends and a carrot-shaped green pompon; on the larger hat of c.1811 the latter had a scarlet tuft at the top. During the Restoration and 'Hundred Days' the hat was apparently quite plain.

The Chasseurs' coat, changing in cut like that of the Grenadiers, was distinguished by white light

Martinet print of a Chasseur officer; note double tassel on the front of the cap.

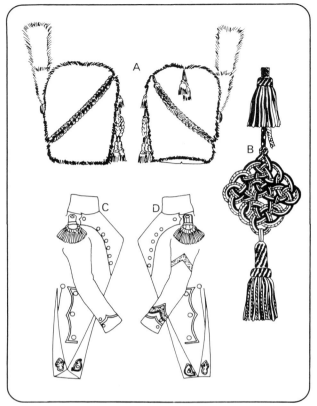

(A) Cap, Chasseurs à Pied—rear at left, front at right. Black fur, with plaited cords, and the two tassels always worn by the Chasseurs. The plume of scarlet over green is in the proportions seen from c.1806; hemispherical cockade, c.1806–08 to 1811. (B) NCO's *raquette*, Chasseurs à Pied. The knot itself was made of woven cords in green (solid shading here), scarlet (light shading here) and gold. The upper tassel had gold fringing overlaid on green; the lower tassel, gold overlaid on scarlet. The ordinary cords of green and scarlet were 'speckled' with gold. (C) Chasseur's coat, with turnbacks of c.1808–10. Blue, with scarlet cuffs, lining, turnback and pocket piping; white lapels and cuff piping; green epaulettes with red fringe, crescent and *bride*; orange-on-white turnback badges. (D) Sergeant, Chasseurs, c.1810–15, with restyled turnbacks. Colouring as above, but gold rank chevron edged scarlet; gold service chevron on upper left sleeve; epaulettes with gold edging and crescent and gold fringe overlaid on scarlet.

September 1803, described as blue in 1804—white linen trousers were used on the march in summer and blue cloth in winter. Greatcoats (first issued in December 1805, according to Barrès, and 'very welcome, for the cloth smocks in which we had made the campaign were neither warm nor handsome') were like those of the Grenadiers but with epaulette retaining straps originally green, red in 1805–06 and blue in 1814–15; and in 1813–15 at least, there was red piping on collar and cuffs.

Equipment was as for Grenadiers, but belts without stitched edges were still in store in 1805. The original sword knot was green with a red knot,

but from 1802–03 had a white leather strap, green knot and red fringe (Otto shows red knot and green fringe). Some old Consular Guard sabres were still in use in September 1804 as well as the new Guard pattern; the cartridge boxes originally bore brass horn badges but from 1806 a crowned eagle. The NCOs' rank badges were like those of the Grenadiers, but in the form of inverted 'V's matching the shape of the cuff; NCOs' cap cords were mixed gold and green until 1806, and gold, green and red thereafter, the frontal tassels remaining gold and green. The amount of gold used in the cords was presumably reduced in about 1811, as the cost was reduced by ten per cent. Hat 'ties' were mixed green and gold. The NCOs' original sword knot had a green strap edged gold, a red and gold knot, and a green fringe with an upper layer of gold; later it had a white leather strap, green and gold knot, and red fringe with gold outer layer. Sergeants' epaulettes had gold lace edging and gold crescent, and from c.1806 a layer of gold fringe over the red; sergeant-majors' epaulettes were similar, but always had an upper layer of gold fringe, and a double layer after 1806. Officers' distinctions were like those of the Grenadiers, but with a hunting-horn as well as a grenade on the epaulette strap, and hunting horns on the gorget and waist belt plate until replaced by the eagle.

During the Restoration, Royal symbols replaced the Imperial (buttons and badges delivered on 5 November 1814), but Imperial ones were substituted during the 'Hundred Days'. Some 6,000 small grenade and horn badges were also delivered, presumably for the corners of the cartridge boxes like those of the Grenadiers. It was observed that during the 'Hundred Days' not more than 20 members of the 3rd and 4th Chasseurs could be found dressed alike.

Drummers wore mixed green and gold lace, as for Plate E3; scarlet 'swallows'-nest' wings with green and gold lace were worn before 1808; transverse epaulette straps were gold, edged green, in 1802–05, and edged scarlet thereafter; and the *brandenbourgs* were removed after 1811. The musicians dressed as Plate C3, with five *brandenbourgs* on the lapels, increased to seven after March 1808. The drum-major was dressed similarly, but with scarlet instead of crimson facings, and wings with gold fringe until 1808. The hat had a green upright plume over a tricolour '*panache*' and scallop-edged lace; the green baldric had gold lace and oakleaf embroidery, costing 1,740 F.; the sabre was carried upon a white leather waist belt with gold lace and oakleaf embroidery, with a gilt rectangular plate bearing a hunting horn, costing 710 francs.

Dutch Grenadiers

The Dutch Grenadiers retained the uniform of the old Royal Guard of Holland. Originally formed in July 1806, this included both Grenadiers and Chasseurs, and though it was composed exclusively of Grenadiers from 1808 onwards the old Chasseur uniform may have lingered for some time. The coat was white with crimson collar, cuffs, turnbacks, lapels, lining and pocket piping, and white cuff flaps. In Dutch service the cuffs had borne no flaps and the lapels had yellow *brandenbourgs* or pointed-ended loops; the latter were removed when the unit was incorporated into the Imperial Guard, but it is unclear exactly when cuff flaps were adopted. Apart from colouring, the uniform followed French Grenadier lines, including red epaulettes, brass buttons, and yellow grenade turnback badges; the undress *surtout* was white with crimson collar and turnbacks and piping on the pockets, cuffs and down the breast; the hat had a yellow loop and 'ties' and a red carrot-pompon. The NCOs' and officers' distinctions were similar in design to those of the French Grenadiers, though both officers' gorgets and waist belt plates are shown as silver with gilt devices, as well as the reverse; officers' epaulettes were gold with grenade badges, and crimson 'lights' for subalterns. The Chasseurs had worn uniforms of the same colouring but with pointed-ended light infantry lapels, green epaulettes with red crescents, red plume with green tip, and short gaiters, which may conceivably have been worn for a short time in Imperial service until new uniforms were issued.

Apart from the uniform colour, the most distinctive feature of the Dutch Grenadiers' uniform was their cap, which had no plate but a crimson rear patch bearing a white grenade (gold for officers); white cords, red plume, and, uniquely, brass chinscales, which had apparently not been worn in Dutch service but are shown thereafter. The greatcoats of 'dark sky-blue' (*bleu céleste foncé*)

were worn in Holland and were again ordered in April 1811; their marching trousers were 'iron grey' (*gris de fer*).

The Dutch band (30 drummers, 20 fifers, 14 musicians, a *chef de musique*, two *tambour-maîtres* and the 6ft 6ins-tall drum-major, Siliakus) retained their sky-blue uniform with yellow facings when incorporated in the Imperial Guard, though it is not certain at what date the busby shown in Plate G2 was worn; otherwise there was a bicorn hat with scalloped silver lace edging, white plume, and alternate red, white and sky-blue feather edging. Drummers (probably only those attached to the band) wore the fur grenadier cap (with white over sky-blue plume) and the sky-blue uniform, with red epaulettes; and the drum-major had the customary additional lace. 'Company' drummers wore the

Chasseur on the march: print from *Recueil des costumes de l'ex-Garde* **(Paris, 1819), by Nicholas-Toussaint Charlet. Although not exactly contemporary, Charlet had served in the Napoleonic Wars (he fought at Clichy Gate in the defence of Paris in 1814), and knew his subject, even though he tended to over-romanticise it. The old Chasseur wears his greatcoat open for ease of movement; note the somewhat battered hat, and the metal water flask.**

Grenadier (left) and Chasseur of the Dutch Royal Guard, c.1809: print after H. Boisselier from the Bucquoy series. This shows the early uniform possibly retained briefly after incorporation into the Imperial Guard: white coat with red collar, cuffs, lapels, lining and turnbacks; yellow loops on collar and lapels; white cap cords. The Grenadier has a scarlet plume and epaulettes; the Chasseur, a scarlet plume tipped green, green epaulettes with scarlet crescents, and the traditional light infantry features of pointed cuffs, lapels and gaiters.

white uniform with red epaulettes, and yellow lace (including *brandenbourgs*) on the collar, cuffs and lapels. Lapel-loops are shown either pointed-ended or tasselled. The Carl Collection shows a Negro musician wearing an oriental costume of a silver-laced red fez with white pagri; a yellow sleeved waistcoat with pointed cuffs laced with Austrian knots; a sky-blue bolero laced white, including 'swallows'-nest' wings; white *seroual* (mameluke-style baggy trousers), red shoes and cummerbund, and an oriental sabre slung from a shoulder belt worn beneath the bolero. Other recorded band uniforms include, from the Carl Collection, a crimson coat with white facings and yellow/gold lace, presumably worn before the regiment was absorbed into the Imperial Guard. By mid- to late 1811 a new musicians' uniform of dark blue with

crimson facings had been ordered, still with gold lace; but it was probably only worn on rare occasions, if at all, as it can only have been delivered shortly before the Russian campaign.

Sapeurs had the same uniform distinctions as the French Grenadier *sapeurs*, though the Carl Collection shows the crimson coat with white facings as worn by the band; and similarly a blue coat, faced crimson, was ordered in 1811 to replace the existing *sapeurs*' uniform of white, faced crimson.

* * *

Firearms

The Consular Guard had its own pattern of musket, with a raised cheek-piece, lock with patent pan cover, and brass fittings including a butt plate with a grenade-shaped finial set into the top of the butt. 1,600 of this type were ordered on 26 February 1797, and on 28 November 1799 a further supply was commissioned. New muskets were distributed in 1802, no longer with the raised cheek-piece or patent pan, but retaining the brass fittings which characterised Guard muskets throughout the era. A development on the *An IX* model, the Guard musket had an overall length of 152cm (barrel 113.7cm); the calibre was 1.75cm, and the weight 4.5kg. Chasseurs were armed with a slightly lighter version with an overall length of 144cm. A later development was a reinforced ramrod channel with beak-shaped rim. Some 9,000 muskets of this pattern were produced between Year IX and 1812, the date of the last production; obviously, in times of difficulty, Line-pattern muskets must have been pressed into service.

Veterans

The Old Guard's Veteran Company was formed on 12 July 1801, for men 'who by reason of age or infirmity were unable to remain on active duty'; they continued to wear a version of Grenadier uniform, with a *surtout* and a bicorn instead of the fur bonnet, red lapels and blue cuff flaps on the *habit*. They continued to draw the pay and privileges of the active Guardsmen, and performed with their old resolve at the siege of Paris, in which they defended the bridge at Neuilly crying, 'The Old Guard has never laid down its arms.' They were allowed to keep their weapons and magazine by the terms of surrender, and continued in existence even under the monarchy. The Veteran Company of the Dutch Grenadiers, which was used to guard the Palace at Amsterdam, wore the uniform shown in Plate G3.

Sources

In addition to the usual contemporary pictures and extant items of equipment, the work of certain non-contemporary artists is recommended, in particular Lucien Rousselot (*L'Armée Française*), J. Onfroy de Bréville ('Job'), Albert Rigondaud ('Rigo'), and the artists of the Bucquoy series, some of whose work may be found in *Les Uniformes du Premier Empire: La Garde Impériale* (E. L. Bucquoy, ed. L.-Y. Bucquoy & G. Devautour, Paris 1977). Histories of the Imperial Guard include *La Garde Impériale* (L. Fallou, Paris 1901); *Histoire anecdotique, politique et militaire de la Garde Impériale* (E. Marco de St. Hilaire, Paris 1847); and, most accessible, the magnificent *Anatomy of Glory* (H. Lachouque & A. S. K. Brown, London 1962), which is the English adaptation of Lachouque's *Napoléon et la Garde Impériale*. Basic details of successive changes in organisation and equipment are listed in *Guide à l'usage des Artistes et Costumiers . . . Uniformes de l'Armée Française* (H. Malibran, Paris 1904, reprinted Krefeld 1972); and the Guard's Colours are detailed in *Drapeaux et Etendards de la Révolution et de l'Empire* (P. Charrié, Paris 1982). Among numerous memoirs by members of the Old Guard, two outstanding examples are available in translation: *The Note-Books of Captain Coignet* (J.-R. Coignet, London 1928), and *Memoirs of a Napoleonic Officer* (J.-B. Barrès, London 1925).

The Plates

A1: Officer, Grenadiers, Consular Guard, 1800
Based upon a print by Alexis Chataignier, this figure has one of several recorded versions of the Consular Guard cap plate, here with 'straight' sides and bearing a silvered grenade. Other features of the Chataignier original—white collar piping and equally spaced buttons on the lapels—would appear to be errors by the artist, though a tassel

shown hanging at the right side of the cap may not be so.

A2: Drummer, Grenadiers, Consular Guard, 1800
This figure, based upon an illustration by Nicolaus Hoffman, shows the early full dress of Grenadier drummers, including both gold lace (on collar, cuffs and wings) and orange-red lace elsewhere, with pointed-ended button-loops and the classic 'swallows'-nest' style wings, as worn until 1808. The cap has the alternative Consular Guard plate with 'wavy' sides, and although an original by Hoffman apparently shows a mauvish-coloured cord (with gold frontal tassel), the colour is apparently intended to be red. The original shows one of several varieties of drum-hoop design, in this case white with blue grenades and intersecting lines.

Grenadier of the Dutch Regiment in the uniform worn when incorporated into the Imperial Guard—white, with red facings and epaulettes, scarlet plume and white cap cords. Print by Martinet.

Drummers, drum-major and musicians of the Dutch Grenadiers. Although not contemporary, this print shows the busby worn with the musicians' sky-blue coat with yellow facings and silver lace. The drum-major's silver-laced baldric is red. His epaulettes alone cost 296 francs! Though often shown plain red, drummers' and *sapeurs'* dress epaulettes must have been much more elaborate than normal—they cost 25 francs, as against 16 francs for sergeants' and 4 francs for corporals' and grenadiers' epaulettes.

The drummers played a role of vital importance to the morale of the Guard. Coignet recalled that at Austerlitz, when the band (at Napoleon's orders and 'contrary to custom') remained in the centre of the unit playing '*On va leur percer le flanc*', the drummers 'beat a charge loud enough to break their drumheads in. The drums and music mingled together. It was enough to make a paralytic move forward.'

A3: Sapeur, Chasseurs, Consular Guard, 1801
Based upon a print published 'chez Jean', this early *sapeur* uniform includes the traditional features of

(A) Uniform of the Negro musician of the Dutch Grenadiers. The yellow, sleeved waistcoat fastened with hooks and eyes, and was edged with white/silver lace; the yellow cuffs and collar had lace decoration. The sky-blue bolero jacket had 'swallows'-nest' wings, and was edged with white/silver lace with cord tracery on the inner edges; there were tassels at the front corners. The scarlet fez had silver 'wolf-tooth' lace round the top, and a white turban fastened by a silver (?) buckle. This uniform was worn with a crimson waist sash and ankle-length baggy trousers (*seroual*), with crimson ankle boots.
(B) Drummer, Dutch Grenadiers, c.1810. Sky-blue coat; yellow collar, lapels, turnbacks, lining, pocket piping, cuffs and flaps; white/silver lace and decorations, including point-ended loops; scarlet epaulettes. Worn with a fur cap with a white-over-sky-blue plume, this uniform was probably restricted to band drummers; ordinary company drummers wore the normal white uniform faced red, with the addition of yellow lace. **(C)** Musician, Dutch Grenadiers, c.1810. As above, but with silver lace, including tassel-ended *brandenbourgs*, and silver trefoil epaulettes on yellow backing.

leather apron and gauntlets, axe and case, and full beard, the latter a compulsory feature for *sapeurs*; Coignet's beard was something of a spectacle, no less than 13 inches long! The cap illustrated apparently has a rear patch, and green cords and *raquettes*, the latter hanging at the rear, a fashion apparently not unique at this early period. Plain green epaulettes are somewhat unusual. The axe-case bears a brass crossed-axes badge, which is repeated (with the addition of a hunting horn) upon the belt and, in cloth, upon the sleeves.

A4: Grenadier, Garde du Directoire, 1797
This figure wears what is virtually the uniform of a *grenadier* of a demi-brigade of Line infantry, but for the white cuff flap. The fur cap was also of Line

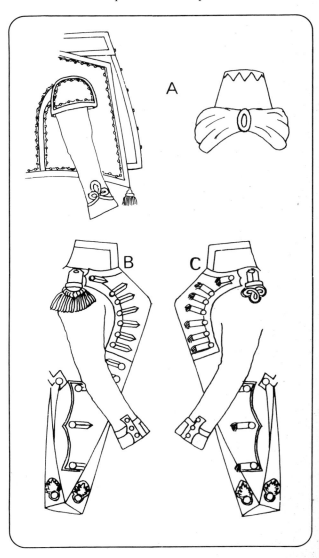

pattern, including the red cords, which may conceivably have been replaced by yellow cords before the adoption of the white.

B1: Officer, Grenadiers, full dress, 1805
This figure, wearing the magnificent full dress of the Guard, is based upon a well-known Martinet print which depicts the use of white gaiters, though breeches and boots would probably have been more common (and, for walking-out dress, breeches with silk stockings and buckled shoes, and the bicorn hat instead of the fur bonnet). As was customary, the cut-feather plumes worn by officers are often depicted as even more magnificent than those of the other ranks, though the difference in rank was not always marked; *Vélite* Barrès, for example, re-marked with pride that though only an ordinary soldier he managed to acquire an officer's cap! Plumes worn by senior officers, of the white colour which normally signified headquarters staff, were usually of the upright *aigrette* variety rather than of cut feathers. The full dress uniform depicted here, worn by the entire regiment, is described with pride by Coignet, who admits: 'We were splendid to look at, but abominably uncomfortable!'

B2: Vélite, full dress, 1805
After an illustration by Hoffman, the *Vélite* uniform illustrated resembles that of the ordinary *grenadiers*, but with blue cuff flaps piped white and blue shoulder straps piped red, and a bicorn worn instead of the bonnet (some sources indicate the use of red plumes). Similar shoulder straps were probably worn upon the *surtout*, which in other respects resembled that of the *grenadiers* or *chasseurs*; but Barrès notes that when he was admitted to the Chasseur-Vélites in 1804, his *surtout* was lined and piped scarlet, his bicorn yellow-laced, his epaulettes were green with red trimming, and he soon afterwards wore the fur bonnet. Coignet remarks upon an ingenious aid to the instruction of company drill: he used 200 little wooden soldiers both to teach himself and, no doubt, his pupils.

B3: Sergeant-major, Grenadiers, summer walking-out dress (Tenue de Sortie), 1805
This figure wears the ordinary walking-out dress, consisting of the ordinary *habit* (still at this period with the more voluminous skirts, the turnbacks not

Drummer, Dutch Grenadiers: print after H. Boisselier from the Bucquoy series, based on the '*Collections Alsaciennes*'. This is the enigmatic crimson uniform with white collar, lapels, cuffs, flaps, lining and turnbacks, apparently worn by the *tête de colonne* in c.1809–10 (?). Scarlet plume and epaulettes, white cap cords, gold lace; brass drum, light blue hoops.

yet 'streamlined'), bicorn hat, breeches, stockings and buckled shoes. As Coignet describes, sergeants were allowed to carry an épée and cane for walking-out dress like the officers, as they ranked with lieutenants of the Line. Lower ranks wore the same costume but carried the ordinary *briquet* (sabre) on a shoulder belt.

C1: Drum-major, Grenadiers, 1804
Based upon an illustration by Nicolaus Hoffman, this figure illustrates the magnificence of the Grenadier drum-major's costume as worn for full dress, among the richest and most expensive uniforms devised during the entire period. Though less elaborate uniforms were worn on active service, they invariably included gold-laced facings, gold epaulettes and the customary sergeant-major's rank bars. The *tambour-maîtres* or *caporaux-tambours* wore a less elaborate though similar uniform, including gold-laced facings with pointed-ended loops on the

Sapeurs **of the Dutch Grenadiers: print after Boisselier. The left-hand man wears the last uniform ordered for the** *tête de colonne,* **of dark blue faced with crimson. The others wear white faced with crimson. Scarlet plumes, white cords; gold and crimson epaulettes; gold badges, backed crimson.**

lapels. One contemporary source indicates a white shoulder belt bearing a gilt grenade badge and supporting an ordinary sabre with gold knot, and a gold-laced bicorn worn 'fore-and-aft' with a red plume. The latter was also worn by the drum-major at a later date, as were hussar boots of a more conventional style than the laced variety shown. For much of the period the drum-major of the Grenadiers was the legendary Sénot, a huge and imposing figure who had been a captain in the Royal army and who later became a lieutenant in the 2nd Grenadiers.

C2: Cymbalist, Grenadiers, 1804

This figure is again taken from Hoffman—but a second version of the same picture, also painted by the artist himself, shows a sky-blue cap with an upright black feather and five white ones each with a sky-blue and red patch; shorter coat skirts without

turnbacks; sky-blue lining; gold shoulder straps edged red; and a silver-fringed sash. As noted before, the Chataignier version of the Negro cymbalist of the Grenadier band depicts a totally different costume.

C3: Musician, Chasseurs, 1808

The Chasseurs' version of the classic Old Guard musicians' uniform varied from that of the Grenadiers by its light infantry cut (pointed-ended lapels and pointed cuffs) and by its colouring, the hat having an edging of green and white feathers and the lapels being white. As described before, the musicians wore five *brandenbourgs* upon each lapel until March 1808, when the number was increased to the usual seven. Each of the Guard musicians was a virtuoso, and (excluding the percussionists) each owned his own instrument and was responsible for its maintenance.

D1: Chasseur, campaign dress, 1807

This figure is basically as shown in the Otto MS, a collection of contemporary watercolours (possibly by C.-F. Weiland) executed for Major Otto in Wiesbaden. The 1806–07 campaign uniform is depicted, comprising fur cap and *surtout*, though the Otto MS appears to be in error in showing more buttons on the breast of the *surtout* than actually existed. As mentioned before, the Otto MS shows a rear patch on the Chasseur cap (probably the latest date at which this questionable feature is recorded), and includes a suggestion of red edging to the epaulette strap; where the latter appears in contemporary pictures it represents not a piping but only the epaulette lining. Among the most distinguished of the Chasseurs of this period was Jean-Claude Depold of the 1st Battalion, who took over a 12-pdr fieldpiece at Wagram, the successful defence of the position being attributed to his 'industry and courage . . . in the face of sharp attacks'.

D2: Officer, Grenadiers, marching order, 1807

This figure wears typical *tenue de route*, including a bicorn instead of the bonnet, and displays the common style of wearing a rolled greatcoat over one shoulder, which not only contained personal possessions within the roll but served as a rudimentary defence against sabre cuts. The *surtout* was equally popular on campaign; the Otto MS shows it worn by an officer with the fur cap (and a black leather waist belt), though the red piping sometimes shown was probably nothing more than the lining becoming visible due to stretching with wear.

D3: Grenadier, campaign dress, 1807
Based upon a Boersch figure, the exact date of this greatcoated grenadier is uncertain; Rousselot thought it a late example, perhaps 1811–14. It is especially interesting in showing a *vieux moustache* (with three service chevrons) wearing a coat which has both collar patch and piping, neither apparently regulated officially; and striped ticking trousers which apparently match the fabric used to cover the bonnet, carried atop the knapsack. New issues of the bicorn continued in use on campaign even after the mass destruction of hats in 1809.

D4: Grenadier, campaign dress, 1807
As shown by Otto, this figure depicts the rear of the

ordinary equipment, worn here with the *surtout*. The whole assemblage was similar to that used by the Line infantry. One shoulder belt supported the cartridge box on the right hip, and the other a combined frog holding both the sabre- and bayonet-scabbards. Larger knapsacks than normal in the Line were usually carried by the Guard. The cap decorations, excluding the frontal tassel which was stitched into place, were usually removed on campaign except when action was imminent.

E1: Chasseur, full dress, 1805
This illustrates the early Chasseur uniform of the classic light infantry cut, before the re-styling of the lapels and turnbacks and before the changes in the colouring of epaulettes, plume, etc., and while the cartridge box still bore the hunting horn badge of the light infantry. Despite the Otto figure having only a single tassel at the front of his plateless cap, it

Napoleon's farewell to the Guard at Fontainebleau, 19 April 1814: engraving after Horace Vernet. Napoleon is embraced by General Petit while Lieutenant Fortin, bearing the 'Eagle' of the 1st Grenadiers, hides his face in emotion.

'Royal Grenadiers'—former Imperial Guardsmen, 1814–15, wearing uniforms virtually unchanged apart from the substitution of white cockade and the removal of Imperial insignia. The cartridge box cover has a large central grenade replacing the eagle. Print by Charlet, from *Costumes Militaires* (Paris, 1817).

seems that the Chasseurs always wore two.

E2: Corporal, Grenadiers, full dress, 1808

The corporal illustrated wears another example of the magnificent but 'abominably uncomfortable' dress uniform of the Grenadiers; note the white gaiters with white garters and buttons, and white gloves, worn in parade dress. Surprisingly, Coignet records that at one time there was a shortage in the Guard of NCOs' rank distinctions, so that when he was promoted to sergeant he had to hand his corporal's stripes to the man who succeeded him, in the meantime wearing no rank markings himself despite his appointment. But after Essling there was no longer any shortage, for his platoon collected stripes and epaulettes from the uniforms of the dead, and soon Coignet had 'pockets full'.

E3: Drummer, Chasseurs, full dress, 1808

This figure shows the uniform of Old Guard drummers following the removal of the 'wings'; drummers of Grenadiers were dressed in a similar fashion, but with their own regimental distinctions of cap, uniform-cut, and red and gold lace. Grenadiers' drums at this period are usually shown with grenade badges upon the shells, and light blue hoops with or without grenades upon them. The drum belts included a rectangular plate with tubes affixed into which the drumsticks fitted, and are usually shown with the regiment's distinctive badge (in this case a horn) higher up the belt. Not all drummers were equipped identically; e.g. drummer Estienne of the Chasseurs, known as 'the drummer of Arcola', was a *légionnaire d'honneur* who used his own, silver-mounted 'drumsticks of honour'.

E4: Grenadier in smock, 1808

The grenadier illustrated shows the design of forage cap and smock (*sarreau*) worn with blue or white trousers in *tenue de corvée*, though the waistcoat could be worn instead. Coignet notes that before Dorsenne imposed stricter discipline troops usually paraded for roll-call wearing only their shirts and breeches, without even stockings!

F1: Sergeant, Chasseurs, full dress, 1810

This shows the later version of Chasseurs' full dress which followed that depicted in Plate E1, with NCO rank distinctions in the form of bars on the sleeves, epaulettes and distinctive cap cords. The latter consisted of a strand of red and a strand of green cord, both with gold interwoven, but the *raquettes* were woven of equally-sized strands of red, gold and green.

F2: Lieutenant Porte-Aigle, 1st Grenadiers, 1811

Successive designs of Colour and 'Eagles' are shown and described in the black-and-white illustrations, but during the Empire period they followed the basic styles in general use with the remainder of the army. Even after the number of 'Eagles' was reduced to one per regiment, battalion numbers continued to be carried on the flag. Exact details of the colour-belts used by the *Porte-Aigles* are uncertain, the existing illustrations apparently being reconstructions; but they were basically scarlet for Grenadiers and green for Chasseurs, with

gold lace edging and gold embroidery, perhaps with gold fringing for the Consular Guard (as shown by Potrelle), and perhaps bearing gilt regimental badges. The 'Eagles' of the Guard were regarded with even greater devotion than those of the Line; at Plancenoit Gen. Pelet grabbed that of the 1st Chasseurs crying, 'To me, Chasseurs, to me! Save the Eagle or die round it!' The remnants of the 2nd Chasseurs formed a hedge of bayonets around it, saving both the 'Eagle' and themselves. At Eylau a shell smashed the 'Eagle'-staff of the 1st Battalion of the 1st Grenadiers; its bearer, Lt. Morlay, picked up the broken pole and jammed it into the muzzle of a musket, carrying it like that for the rest of the day.

F3: Sapeur, Grenadiers, full dress, 1810
This figure wears the full dress *sapeur* uniform with the additional lace, including on the sleeve seams, which was apparently introduced around 1810. Contemporary sources show a variety of versions of cap cords, epaulettes and badges used by Guard *sapeurs*. Potrelle shows for the Consular Guard cords of mixed white and gold; Hoffman shows gold, Otto

'Napoleon at Waterloo'—watercolour by Charles Steuben, showing the Emperor sheltering inside a square of the Grenadiers à Pied.

mixed red and silver, and Martinet white. Similarly, epaulettes range from those laced in the manner of sergeants to others shown plain red. Sleeve badges are shown variously to consist of red crossed axes (Otto, on the *surtout*); white axes edged red (Martinet); gold axes edged white (Potrelle); or gold grenade over axes with or without a lower grenade, those on the left sleeve superimposed upon service chevrons where applicable. Another version shows the use of pistols carried in loops on the waist belt, presumably carried in place of the usual carbine; and various patterns of sabre were used, as shown in the black-and-white illustrations.

G1: Corporal, 3rd Grenadiers, full dress, 1811
This shows the uniform of the Dutch Grenadiers after the removal of the *brandenbourgs* from the lapels, and with the addition of cuff flaps—though the date at which the flaps were added is uncertain, as most of the contemporary pictures show the

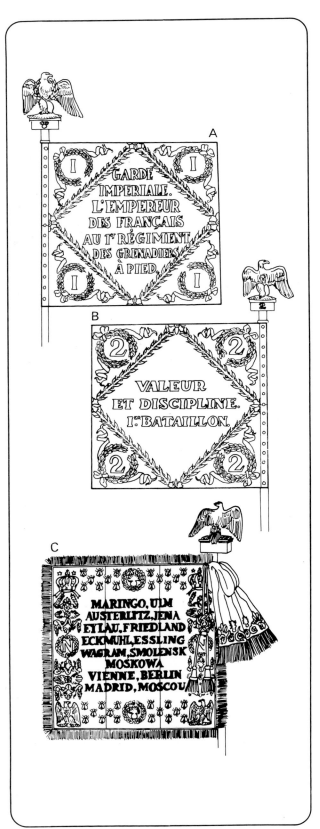

(A) 'Eagle', 1st Grenadiers, 1811 issue of 1804 pattern. White central diamond; corner triangles blue (top left, bottom right) and red; all decorations gold. Dimensions, 80cm square. Gilded Eagle. The 1804 issue was similar but for the inscription 'DE GRENADIERS' instead of 'DES GRENADIERS'; and the number '1' on the 'Eagle' plinth. Two 1804 pattern 'Eagles' were presented to the 1st Grenadiers on 5 December 1804, and two to the 1st Chasseurs on 5 September. One each of the 1811 issue was presented to the 3rd Grenadiers (30 June 1811), and to the 1st and 2nd Grenadiers and 1st and 2nd Chasseurs on 15 August 1811. There is no evidence that the 2nd Grenadiers and 2nd Chasseurs of 1806-09 ever received 'Eagles'. The inscription on the reverse was as (B) below.

(B) Reverse of 'Eagle' of 2nd Chasseurs, 1811 issue of 1804 pattern. Generally colours as above, but note blue triangles top right, bottom left. Inscription on obverse as (A) above, with obvious difference of regimental title. Corner numbers indicated regiment, not battalion. The use of the inscription 'L^{er} BATAILLON' continued even after reduction of 'Eagles' from one per battalion to one per regiment. Staff usually blue; flag fixed with gilded studs.

(C) Reverse of 'Eagle', 1st Grenadiers, 1812 pattern. Tricolour—blue nearest staff, white, red. All decorations and fringe, gold. *Cravate* of vertical tricolour bands, gold embroidery and cords. The obverse bore the inscription 'GARDE/IMPERIALE/L'EMPEREUR/NAPOLEON/AU 1er REGIMENT/DES GRENADIERS/A PIED'. The other decorations were identical to the reverse. Note unusual spelling of 'MARINGO'. Dimensions, 82cm square. The pattern was received in April 1813 by the 1st and 2nd Grenadiers, and in May by the 1st and 2nd Chasseurs (these, with horns probably replacing the grenades).

'Eagles' were issued in 1815 to the 1st Grenadiers and Chasseurs only; these were destroyed in September 1815, but were probably of similar design to the 1813 issue above—although they may conceivably have borne battle-honours on both sides, as did the standard of the Guard Artillery, which still exists. The 'Eagle' of the 1st Chasseurs was apparently carried at Waterloo by the regiment's 2nd Bn., and was used to rally the 2nd Chasseurs.

sleeves positioned in such a way that the flap, or its absence, is not visible! The equipment, legwear, etc., resemble those of the French Grenadiers; but note the yellow lace rank bars and service chevrons, and the distinctive fur bonnet without a plate but with the unusual addition of chinscales.

G2: Musician, Dutch Grenadiers, full dress, 1810
The date of the use of the busby by the band of the Dutch Grenadiers is uncertain; it may perhaps have pre- or post-dated 1810. It is likely that the band usually wore the bicorn hat, with scalloped silver lace edging; silver 'ties' and loop; red, white and sky-blue feather edging, and white plume, with the sky-blue uniform as well as with the (presumably) earlier crimson version, and the later dark blue band uniform with crimson facings. Though the drum-major wore the sky-blue band uniform with yellow facings, and presumably also the busby, sky-blue was probably only worn by those drummers attached to the band; 'company' drummers would have worn the ordinary white uniform with crimson facings and yellow lace, including *brandenbourgs*. The brass drum-shells bore grenade badges, the

sky-blue hoops having gilt grenades.

G3: Veteran, 3rd Grenadiers, 1812
The veteran illustrated wears the uniform of the company which guarded the Palace at Amsterdam; basically the *tenue de ville* of the ordinary Dutch Grenadiers, consisting of the bicorn hat, and a *surtout* in regimental colouring—white with crimson/red collar, lining, turnbacks and epaulettes, and red piping on the vertical pockets and around the white cuffs.

G4: Guimbardier, 3rd Grenadiers, campaign dress, 1812
The figure illustrated represents one of the 12 regimental *guimbardiers* (drivers of regimental transport waggons) attached to the Dutch Grenadiers; the uniform is a reconstruction after Boisselier, as their exact costume is unknown. The man illustrated wears the regimental sky-blue greatcoat; and it is known that the *guimbardiers* were equipped with shakos costing 9 F. each.

H1: Sergeant, Grenadiers, campaign dress, 1812–15
Campaign dress towards the end of the Empire tended to become increasingly bizarre, as official supplies ran out and all manner of captured or looted clothing and equipment was pressed into service. Nevertheless, the Guard always maintained as uniform an appearance as possible; the main exception was during the retreat from Moscow, when the use of civilian clothes and tattered uniforms led to the whole army resembling 'phantoms in carnival masks', in the words of Col. Griois of the Guard Artillery. The *vieux moustache* illustrated here retains a 'regulation' appearance—though the use of hats, bonnets with cords and plumes removed, and the possible use of single-breasted greatcoats (as common in the Line) and trousers of blue, white or ochre tended to disrupt total uniformity. The sergeant wears a plain greatcoat (devoid of piping, unlike some recorded examples from this period), with the epaulettes and bars of his rank attached. Note also the mixed scarlet and gold hat decorations worn by NCOs. A common practice was to wear a rectangle of red ribbon sewn to the left breast as an alternative to displaying the cross of the *Légion d'Honneur*.

H2: Officer, Grenadiers, campaign dress, 1812–15

'La Garde Meurt': wreathed in the smoke of battle, an 'Eagle' is raised in defiance over the last stand of the Old Guard at Waterloo. Print after Hippolyte Bellangé, 1849.

The officer illustrated wears the *surtout*, popular for use on campaign. The epaulettes are allowed to hang loose onto the breast, so as to be visible in the opening of the greatcoat. This could vary in colour from blue to brown or grey for officers. Some pictures suggest that the bicorn hat, worn 'fore-and-aft' (*en colonne*), could have the cockade loop turned to either side.

H3: Sergeant-major, Chasseurs, undress, 1812–15
This shows the use of the *surtout* with the hat, winter breeches and 'Suvarov' boots, with NCO rank distinctions including an officers'-style épée worn with a waist belt, as permitted for Guard NCOs—who kept the *surtout* even though it appears to have been withdrawn from the privates and corporals around 1810.

The veteran sergeant-majors represented perhaps the most stalwart 'old of the Old' who 'didn't give a b.....', as Scheltens wrote. Coignet was typical. He recounts a lucky escape at Essling, when performing his natural functions in no-man's-land between the armies. A roundshot landed nearby, throwing up a shower of stones; 'black and blue behind', he shuffled back to the French line, musket in one hand and trousers in the other. 'That was a near thing', said his captain. 'It was, sir,' replied Coignet; 'their paper's too hard, I couldn't use it'!

H4: Chasseur, marching order, 1815
This figure shows the rear of the equipment as worn in 1815, including a fabric pouch cover bearing the eagle and corner horns and grenades stencilled in black; otherwise, the equipment is virtually the same as that shown in Plate D4. The Chasseur wears the bonnet as on campaign, with cords and plume removed, though the cockade at the left side and the frontal tassel were retained; the long blue trousers were worn over black or white gaiters.

Farbtafeln

A1 Die Uniform beruht zum Teil auf einem Druck von Chataignier: wir haben das Helmschild mit einem versilberten Granatenmotiv übernommen; andere Merkmale wie z.B. die weissen Biesen am Kragen oder der gleichmässige Abstand zwischen den Knöpfen scheinen nicht authentisch zu sein. **A2** Diese auf Hoffman beruhende Paradeuniform aus der Zeit vor 1808 ist mit 'Schwalbennestern' auf den Schultern sowie einer Helmschild-Variation versehen. **A3** Eine interessante, frühe Ausführung der Sapeur-Uniform mit den meisten traditionellen Merkmalen sowie einer interessanten, frühen Helmverzierung. **A4** Dies ist quasi die Uniform eines Grenadiers einer Demi-Brigade der Infanterie.

B1 Die Uniform beruht auf einem Druck von Martinet; der Offizier trägt seine Gamaschen auf ungewöhnliche Weise. Der Federnbusch eines Offiziers war von weit besserer Qualität. **B2** Der Vélite unterschied sich vom Grenadier durch seine blaue Manschettenlasche mit weisser Biese, seinen blauen Schulterstreifen mit roter Biese und seinem Bicord-Helm. **B3** Normale Ausgehuniform; Feldwebel und höhere Ränge trugen einen Epée und einen Rohrstock.

C1 Diese Uniform basiert auf Hoffman. Sie sehen die herrliche Paradeuniform eines Tambourmajors, die mehrere tausend Franc kostete. Der legendäre Sénot war lange Zeit der Tambourmajor; er war vorher ein Offizier der Königlichen Armee und später Leutnant des 2. Grenadiers. **C2** Auch diese Uniform beruht auf Hoffman. Er malte zwei völlig verschiedene Uniformen zu unterschiedlichen Zeiten, von denen keine dem Chataignier-Druck gleicht. **C3** Beachten Sie die für die leichte Infanterie typischen Merkmale wie z.B. spitze Manschetten und Revers sowie grüne Federn.

D1 Grundlage hierfür war die Otto MS mit einigen Ausnahmen wie die Knopfzahl und der Surtout. Otto zeigt ein Abzeichen hinten auf der Mütze, ein eigenartiges Merkmal, das hier zuletzt erfasst wurde. **D2** Während des Feldzuges war der Surtout eine beliebte Alternative zum Habit. Der um den Körper geschlungene, gerollte Mantel enthielt kleine persönliche Gegenstände und diente darüber hinaus als Schutz gegen Schwertverletzungen. **D3** Das Datum ist umstritten; Rousselot glaubte, diese Boersch-Figur ging auf die Zeit von 1811–1814 zurück. Weder die Kragenabzeichen noch die Biesen sind offizielle Merkmale dieses Mantels. **D4** Die persönlichen Gegenstände des Soldaten sind hier von hinten über einen Surtout zu sehen. Die Tornister der Wache waren grösser als die der Frontsoldaten.

E1 Eine frühe Chasseur-Uniform, bevor Revers und Umschlag neu entworfen und die Farben der Epauletten, der Federn usw. geändert wurden. **E2** Ein weiteres Beispiel der grandiosen Paradeuniform, die in Memoiren als 'fürchterlich unbequem' beschrieben wird. **E3** Tambouruniform nach den 1808 vorgenommenen Änderungen; Tambouren der Grenadiers trugen dieselbe Uniform, mit regiments-typischen Unterschieden. **E4** Zur Musiks-uniform gehörten der Bonnet de police und der Sarreau. Anstelle des Rockes trugen die Soldaten auch manchmal die Weste.

F1 Vergleichen Sie diese Uniform mit der Paradeuniform von E1. An einer anderen Stelle wird in diesem Buch die genaue Konstruktion der Raquettes aus grünen, roten und goldenen Kordeln erläutert. **F2** Die Details dieser Trägergürtel der Standartenträger sind umstritten: die der Grenadiers waren im allgemeinen scharlachrot, die der Chasseurs grün mit goldener Verzierung und manchmal auch goldenen Abzeichen. **F3** Die Paradeuniform eines Sapeurs mit zusätzlichen Spitzenverzierung, die ca. 1810 hinzu kam. In zeitge-nössischen Darstellungen sind Epauletten, Ärmelabzeichen usw. sehr unterschiedlich.

G1 Zu dieser Zeit hatte man bereits die Brandenbourgs vom Revers entfernt. Wann die Manschetten umgestaltet wurden und die Lasche hinzu kam, ist ungewiss. Beachten Sie die Kinnriemen am Helm. **G2** Aus welcher Zeit diese Kolpak-Kopfbedeckung aus Fell stammt, steht nicht fest. Sonst trug die Kapelle normalerweise den Bicot-Helm. **G3** Die Kompanie, die den Palast in Amsterdam bewachte, trug im Grunde die Ausgehuniform der 3. Grenadiers —einen Bicot-Helm und einen Surtout in den Regimentsfarben. **G4** Einer von zwölf Transportwagen-Fahrer des Regiments, rekonstruiert nach einem Druck von Boisselier, da die genaue Uniform nicht bekannt ist.

H1 Die Wache trug falls möglich immer eine 'reguläre' Uniform, obwohl die kaiserliche französische Armee in späteren Jahren eine ganze Kollektion verschiedener Uniformen trug. **H2** Die Epauletten dürfen lose vorn auf dem Surtout hängen, so dass sie unter dem offenen Mantel zu sehen sind. **H3** Beachten Sie das Epée-Muster des Offiziers; Die Unteroffiziere der Wache durften es tragen. Die Truppen legten ca. 1810 diesen Surtout ab, aber die Unteroffiziere behielten ihn bei. **H4** Typische Feldzuguniform und Zubehör während der zwielichten Phase des Kaiserreichs.

Notes sur les planches en couleur

A1 Partiellement basé sur une gravure de Chataignier; nous suivons son exemple en montrant ce style d'insigne de bonnet avec un motif de grenade argenté, mais d'autres caractéristiques telles que le passepoil blanc de col et l'écartement égal des boutons semblent être des erreurs. **A2** D'après Hoffman, cette illustration montre des caractéristiques de la tenue réglementaire d'avant 1808, telles que les 'nids d'hirondelle' sur les épaules et une autre variation de l'insigne de bonnet. **A3** Style précoce intéressant de l'uniforme de sapeur, comprenant la plupart des caractéristiques traditionnelles, mais avec des détails intéressants de la décoration du bonnet. **A4** Virtuellement l'uniforme d'un grenadier d'une demi-brigade d'infanterie.

B1 D'après une gravure de Martinet, illustrant un emploi inhabituel de guêtres blanches par un officier. Les plumes des officiers étaient de qualité supérieure. **B2** Les caractéristiques qui distinguaient le Vélite du Grenadier étaient la patte de manchettes liséré de blanc, la patte d'épaule bleue liséré de rouge et le chapeau bicorne. **B3** Tenue normale de sortie avec l'épée et la cane portées par les sergents et les rangs au-dessus.

C1 D'après Hoffman, cette illustration présente le magnifique uniforme de parade du tambour-major, costume qui coûtait plusieurs milliers de francs. Le tambour-major de la plus grande partie de cette période était le légendaire Sénot, un ex-officier de l'armée royale et plus tard lieutenant des 2e Grenadiers. **C2** Egalement d'après Hoffman, cette illustration présente deux uniformes entièrement différents à des périodes différentes et ni l'un ni l'autre ne ressemble à la gravure de Chataignier. **C3** Noter des caractéristiques typiques de l'infanterie légère, telles que les manchettes et les revers pointus et les plumes vertes.

D1 D'après Otto MS, avec quelques corrections telles que le nombre de boutons sur le surtout. Otto présente un écusson arrière sur le bonnet; c'est la dernière date à laquelle cette caractéristique douteuse est notée. **D2** Le surtout était populaire pour remplacer l'habit en campagne. La capote roulée portée autour du corps contenait des petits biens personnels et apportait une certaine protection contre les coups d'épée. **D3** La date est douteuse: Rousselot pensait que ce personnage de Boersch datait de 1811–14. Ni l'écusson de col ni les liserés ne constituaient des caractéristiques officielles de la capote. **D4** Le dos de l'équipement personnel du soldat, vu ici par dessus un surtout. Les sacs d'ordonnance de la Garde étaient plus grands que les sacs distribués aux troupes de ligne.

E1 Uniforme précoce de Chasseur, avant la modification du style des revers et des rabats et le changement de la couleur des épaulettes, des plumes, etc. **E2** Un autre exemple du magnifique habit de parade qui est décrit dans des mémoires comme 'abominablement inconfortable!' **E3** Uniforme de tambour après les modifications de 1808; les tambours Grenadiers portaient le même costume, avec des différences évidentes entre les régiments. **E4** Le bonnet de police et sarreau servent comme uniforme de corvée; le gilet pouvait aussi être porté, au lieu du sarreau.

F1 A comparer avec l'uniforme de parade précédent, illustré par E1. Un schéma contenu dans ce livre se livre présente la construction exacte des raquettes de corde verte, rouge et or. **F2** Les détails des brayers des porte-étendards ne sont pas établis de façon certaine: ceux des Grenadiers étaient essentiellement écarlates, ceux des Chasseurs essentiellement verts, avec des décorations dorées et peut-être des insignes or. **F3** Uniforme de parade du Sapeur, avec la décoration en passement supplémentaire ajoutée vers 1810. Les détails des épaulettes, des insignes de manche, etc sont très variés dans les illustrations contemporaines.

G1 Les brandebourgs avaient été supprimés sur les revers à cette époque; la date exacte à laquelle la manchette a été modifiée pour inclure une patte n'est pas connue. Noter les mentonnières à 'écailles' de métal fixées au bonnet. **G2** La date de cette coiffe *kolpak* est incertaine; le bicorne semble généralement avoir été porté par la fanfare. **G3** Cette compagnie, qui gardait le palais à Amsterdam, portait essentiellement l'uniforme de sortie des 3e Grenadiers—un bicorne et un surtout dans les couleurs du régiment. **G4** Un de douze conducteurs de voitures de transport du régiment, dans une reconstruction d'après Boisselier, le costume exact n'étant pas connu.

H1 La Garde maintenait un aspect le plus 'réglementaire' possible, quoique les dernières années de l'Empire virent les armées françaises porter un ensemble mal assorti d'uniformes. **H2** Il est permis aux épaulettes de tomber sur la poitrine du surtout de façon à être visibles sous l'avant ouvert de la capote. **H3** Noter le type d'épée de l'officier, autorisé pour les sous-officiers de la Garde, et le surtout, conservé par les sous-officiers, après son abandon par les troupes vers 1810. **H4** Equipement et tenue de campagne typiques du crépuscule de l'Empire.